The Death of a Dream

# ENDORSEMENTS

"Despite the popular narrative that we can all achieve our dreams, life rarely works out that way for most of us. While it isn't easy, letting a dream die is the key to finding new opportunities already before you. In this refreshingly honest and vulnerable book, Daron Earlewine offers the disappointments of his journey to save you some grief on your own. It's a hope-filled ride to finding the life God has for you. Don't miss it."

—**Wayne Jacobsen,** co-author of *New York Times* bestselling *The Shack* and author of *Live Loved Free Full.*

"You can do whatever your heart dreams" seems to be a mantra in our culture, but what about when you can't? Or what about when a dream disintegrates or even dies--then what? Daron shares his own story that gives hope for a path forward into an even greater story when it seems like all you've hoped for and dreamt of has died. If you've had the death of a dream, this is a must-read book to give you hope, perspective, and the courage to consider that a dream's death might be the only way for a new dream to be born."

—**John Burke,** *New York Times* bestselling author of *Imagine Heaven*

"Daron has seen his dream die and has found Gods plan for life within that death and his plan for life beyond it in the rebirth of something even greater. He is a trustworthy guide in the broken landscape of dying dreams. Throughout the history of scripture the great male and female heroes all became familiar with the narrative of dreams that die. Abraham and Sarah dreamt of a child, Joseph dreamt of significance, Moses dreamt of freedom for his people, Ruth dreamt of security and David dreamt of being a king.

All of these dreams died and all were given new life by the sovereign grace of God!

This is not a theme common in a contemporary world of 'you can do anything' messaging. And yet, the death of dreams is the experience of so many of us. If you need to understand how God is working in your dreams -whether they are alive or dead - this book is for you."

—**Mike Breen,** Pastor and Author of *Building a Discipling Culture: How to launch a missional movement by discipling people like Jesus did* and *Family On Mission.*

"Daron Earlewine's dynamic, creative, gifted leadership is evident from the moment you meet him. But I've seen that play out over two decades worth of moments, in the real testing ground of real life. Daron has been a catalyst for growth and source of deep encouragement in my life. I'm honored to call him my friend."

—**Matt LeRoy,** co-pastor of Love Chapel Hill, an eclectic, quirky church plant in downtown Chapel Hill, North Carolina and co-author of *Awakening Grace: spiritual practices to transform your soul.*

"I've had dreams come to a dead end and wasn't sure what was next. Daron hits this topic head on with great insight as he invites you in on his discovery through a dream dying and then seeing new ones arise from the gentle nudges that God weaves through our lives.".

—**Justin Masterson,** former Major League Baseball pitcher and 2013 All-Star selection.

"If you've been disappointed by the delay of a dream or devastated by the death of a dream, Daron wrote this book for you... for us. Each chapter feels like you're having coffee with a good friend; learning from his experience, growing from his wisdom. This book will reawaken your courage to dream again."

—**Justin Davis,** Pastor of Hope City Church and best-selling author of *Beyond Ordinary: When a Good Marriage Just Isn't Good Enough*

"Few people I know can communicate like Daron Earlewine. He has an inspiring knack for taking everyday and often humorous observations and weaving them into profound spiritual truths that propel his listeners out of the mundane. He does it over and over as a speaker and podcaster and here he's done it as a writer. The pages of this book will make you laugh, cry, and walk away infused with purpose. We've all experienced the pain of burying a dream. But Daron helps us to see it for what it really is -- a seed that is merely hidden and will come alive anew."

—**Davey Blackburn,** Author of *Nothing is Wasted*, Founder of Nothing is Wasted Ministries, Host of the Nothing is Wasted Podcast.

# DARON EARLEWINE

# THE DEATH OF A DREAM

*Resurrecting Purpose When Life
Doesn't Go As Planned*

NEW YORK

LONDON • NASHVILLE • MELBOURNE • VANCOUVER

# The Death of a Dream

## Resurrecting Purpose When Life Doesn't Go As Planned

Published in New York, New York, by Morgan James Publishing. Morgan James is a trademark of Morgan James, LLC. www.MorganJamesPublishing.com

Proudly distributed by Ingram Publisher Services.

Unless otherwise indicated, all Scripture quotations are taken from *The Message*, copyright © 1993, 2002, 2018 by Eugene H. Peterson. Used by permission of NavPress. All rights reserved. Represented by Tyndale House Publishers, Inc.
Scripture quotations marked NIV are from The Holy Bible, New International Version®, NIV® Copyright © 1973, 1978, 1984, 2011 by Biblica, Inc.® Used by permission. All rights reserved worldwide.
Scripture quotations marked NLT are taken from the *Holy Bible*, New Living Translation, copyright © 1996, 2004, 2015 by Tyndale House Foundation. Used by permission of Tyndale House Publishers, Inc., Carol Stream, Illinois 60188. All rights reserved.
Scripture quotations marked TPT are from The Passion Translation®. Copyright © 2017, 2018, 2020 by Passion & Fire Ministries, Inc. Used by permission. All rights reserved. ThePassionTranslation.com.

**Morgan James BOGO™**

A **FREE** ebook edition is available for you or a friend with the purchase of this print book.

CLEARLY SIGN YOUR NAME ABOVE

**Instructions to claim your free ebook edition:**
1. Visit MorganJamesBOGO.com
2. Sign your name CLEARLY in the space above
3. Complete the form and submit a photo of this entire page
4. You or your friend can download the ebook to your preferred device

ISBN 9781631958755 paperback
ISBN 9781631958762 ebook
Library of Congress Control Number:
2021953355

**Cover Design by:**
Megan Dillon
megan@creativeninjadesigns.com

**Interior Design by:**
Christopher Kirk
www.GFSstudio.com

Morgan James PUBLISHING **Builds** with... **Habitat for Humanity®** Peninsula and Greater Williamsburg

Morgan James is a proud partner of Habitat for Humanity Peninsula and Greater Williamsburg. Partners in building since 2006.

Get involved today! Visit MorganJamesPublishing.com/giving-back

*To: Cole, Ty and Knox. My three sons. I pray this book awakens the dreams of God within you. Never hesitate to trust the heart of the Father. He created you on purpose and for a purpose. He will always be near you. He is always for you. Chase his dreams and become who you were born to be.*

*I love you, Dad*

# ACKNOWLEDGMENTS

To my amazing, loving, wise and loyal wife Julie. After Jesus, you have always been the best decision I have ever made. Thank you for putting up with my dream chasing for over twenty years.

To Dave and Debbie Earlewine, thank you for living loved by God. Your humble, honest and authentic faith have given me an example to imitate and inspired my faith. Thank you for giving my earliest dreams the runways necessary to fly.

To Matt and Hannah Ott, thank you for believing and investing in this project before anyone else did. Without your faith in me and support, this project would never have happened.

To Emily Sutherland, your partnership in this project was everything to me. I would never have found the courage to write this book without your encouragement. There would be no book without your talent. Here's to many more projects together.

To everyone included in the pages of this book. Thank you. I love you.

To my amazing team at Blackbird Mission, thank you for walking this journey with me.

# CONTENTS

# INTRODUCTION

"**T**he Death of a Dream." That sounds like a blast, Daron.

If that's you right now, I get it. I mean, yes, I am inviting you to the funeral of my dream. But not because I'm into depressing stories. I've actually put this book off because I wasn't sure who would read it. But after talking with hundreds of people about their dreams during the past several years, I hear over and over again from people who are devastated because their dreams took them to a dead end and they didn't know what to do next.

I'm writing this story for everyone out there who is in the same boat where I once found myself. I'm writing it to tell you that you are not alone, that your story is far from over, and that there is more to look forward to than you can possibly imagine.

As I begin writing this book, I am hanging out in balmy Arizona while my wife and three boys are freezing in Indiana. (Sorry, honey. I love you. Can't wait to see you at the end of this week.)

I came here because Arizona is "ground zero"—the place where my dream first took root. In between writing sessions, I have been visiting friends who were there when my dream started taking shape. Some of them were even part of it. Being here brings back a lot of emotions and details. I feel all over again how personal and vulnerable my dream was.

Pretty much everyone who has talked to me about their dreams could pinpoint a specific moment when every fiber of their being shouted, "This is what you were born to do!"

If your dream didn't shout, maybe it whispered. Either way, you know what you heard, and it felt amazing.

For many of us, our dreams were born early in life. My friend Heather remembers standing on top of a playground slide, singing at the top of her lungs, and speaking to people who weren't there. She remembers the pure, unadulterated joy she felt in those moments. She was just a little girl, but that was the memory she recalled when I asked about the moment her dream came to life. Years have passed since that day, and Heather is now an outstanding speaker and leader. That day on that playground wasn't her job or career, but something in that moment brought to life the first flickers of a fire of calling. A dream was coming to life.

For others, the dream emerges later in life. My friend Ben was pursuing a career as an opera singer when he was invited to volunteer for an event raising awareness about human trafficking. He didn't even know what the event was about when he agreed to help, but that night changed his life forever. That night a dream died and a purpose was resurrected. Less than one year later, he had launched an organization that now operates in ten countries and has helped free more than 100,000 kids from the atrocities of human trafficking.

No matter when a dream captures your attention, you know when it happens. And when it does, you are forever changed.

I remember the moment my dream was born. I was in the third grade. My brother and I were visiting a local bookstore with our parents. Being the good pastor's kids we were, we bee-lined for the contemporary Christian music section to look for a new cassette tape. For everyone born after 1990, a cassette tape is what we listened to music on before CDs and right after vinyl records. Don't judge me for being old enough to remember this.

At the time, our musical diet was heavy on Carman, David Meece, and a little Petra. If those names are unfamiliar to you, that will be a fun internet search. You're welcome. And remember, old people like me can still serve a purpose.

As Damon and I flipped through all the cassettes looking for one we didn't have yet, *bam!* We spotted an album called *To Hell with the Devil* by Stryper. The cover art was awesome and aggressive, and the band was decked out in spandex outfits with huge eighties hair. We were immediately hooked. We hadn't even heard it yet, but we were convinced we couldn't live without this recording.

We hurried across the store to our parents, holding in our sweaty little hands the coolest thing we had ever seen at that point in our young lives. We begged them in stereo to let us buy it.

"Can we buy it?? Pleeeeease?!!! Come on!!" we pleaded in unison. Their answer was a stone cold "No."

*To Hell with the Devil* by Stryper was not coming home with us that day. But that visit to our local Christian bookstore ignited in me two previously undiscovered talents: the gift of persuasion and, soon thereafter, a passion for playing drums.

My brother and I went home and started formulating a detailed argument to convince our parents of all the reasons why we should be allowed to buy *To Hell with the Devil*. We emphasized the fact that Stryper was actually a Christian band, so naturally this tape would benefit us spiritually. Looking back, I'm not sure what sources we were able to cite. There was no internet back then. But we managed to convince our parents that *To Hell with the Devil* would make us better sons and deepen our spiritual life. Or maybe we just wore them down until they lacked the strength to resist. Either way, they eventually agreed to let us buy it.

We were stoked out of our minds to finally hit Play for the first time. And from the first measure of the first song, my life was forever rocked. That album resounded with my young soul and woke my dream like a sleeping giant I never knew was there. Robert Sweet, the drummer of Stryper, became my hero. I wanted to play like him. I wanted to be like him. I wanted to be him.

Everything in my life at that point, in one way or another, came back to one goal. I would find a way to start a band as cool and groundbreaking as Stryper, and I would spend the rest of my days making awesome music that pointed people to God and rocked other people's worlds like mine had been rocked. That was my dream.

So what's your story? How far back does your dream go? Way back?

Maybe you can relate to the high that comes with discovering what you were born to do. If only our dreams came with warning labels like "The contents of this dream are combustible and may result in getting burned." Truth is, I probably wouldn't have listened, anyway. That dream was everything to me.

I grew up in church, and from birth until I left for college, I heard hundreds of sermons about trusting God with my future and how I had been knit together in my mother's womb for a purpose. Many of those sermons were from my dad. I also heard what happened to people who rebelled against God's path for our lives. Ending up in the digestive tract of a giant fish did not sound cool. And plagues?! No thank you. I'll pass.

Even with all that, I knew—I mean *knew*—if I didn't make my dream happen, my life was going to suck. If God loved me, how would he keep me from doing the only thing that would make me complete?

Spoiler alert: I did not become Robert Sweet. Well, I almost did. And I think that *almost* hurts as much as the death of the dream did. Watching my dream die hurt so badly, I can still taste the tears.

Maybe you've experienced that pain, too. If it's hard to just move on, go easy on yourself. Your dream has been with you for a long time. If it crashes and burns, it's easy to feel like you are burning down with it.

The only reason a dude like me would risk my dignity to share this story is because I hope that, just maybe, through my story you will see your own story emerge. If nothing else, maybe you'll feel understood. Maybe you've even had the same questions and fears I've had.

I have come to believe that our dreams are way more than an exercise in torture. I hope my story helps you see your own gifts, hopes, and future more clearly. This world needs you and all the things you're amazing at. So, together, let's figure out how to rekindle that fire in you.

*Chapter One*

# WORST DAY EVER

You're blessed when you feel you've lost what is most dear to you. Only then can you be embraced by the One most dear to you.

—*Matthew 5:4*

The death of a dream is terrible, even in the best conditions. But mine happened to die in the middle of an Indiana winter.

After spending most of my growing up years in Arizona, I'd developed a love affair with the sun. When I say I love sunshine and warm weather, I actually mean I deeply love it. Maybe it's not the actual sun itself I'm obsessed with, but the effects of the sun. I like suntans and backyard pools. I love everything about big, blue skies full of warm, yellow sun with no clouds, no rain, and little to no humidity. I don't ask much, right? It's just that I really, really like being warm. And I really, really hate being cold.

When I was a kid and dreamed of how my life would go, I naturally assumed my dream would be an Arizona thing, or maybe a California thing. Wherever it was going to happen, it would be a warm thing. So I'm sure you can imagine my reaction when the dream I had been chasing since third grade took me to Indiana. Clearly, I was deeply committed to this dream if I was willing to suffer Midwestern winters for it. Truth is, I would have endured just about anything to make it happen.

To add an extra layer of cruelty, the death of my dream coincided with an ice storm. The destruction of my future wasn't bad enough, so let's add sleet stinging my face. If you've never had the misfortune of walking through a sleet storm, it's basically tiny shards of ice descending from the sky trying to kill people. It's torture.

I wasn't totally unaware of Midwestern winters. I had actually spent the first eight years of my life in the Midwest. But when I was a kid, winter was kind of fun. I mean, there's Christmas in December. And we got snow, which meant snow forts, snowball fights, and sledding, and that's all great. But as I got older, snow was pretty for the first half hour, then it just became annoying to drive in, walk in, and shovel. But I digress.

Up until that sleet-infested day, I was having a blast pursuing my dream with every ounce of energy in me. After pouring more than half of my life into becoming a great drummer, I'd brought this dream to Indiana and formed a band, and it was working. It was really taking off. We played in a lot of cool places, toured, and played for all kinds of amazing events. We were making music that was about something. I really thought we would do big things and make a difference. The fulfillment of my dream was almost within reach.

This dream of being a musician wasn't just about the benefits of rock-star life, although like any ambitious young adult, I wouldn't have opposed fame or fortune. I really just wanted to play drums for the rest of my life. I had started playing shortly after I discovered that first Stryper recording, and I had a knack for it. Not everything came that naturally to me, so I loved every minute that I was playing drums. I pursued music with my whole being. I mean, I had the whole rock-star deal going on: the long hair, the earrings, the whole nine yards.

The band members had become like brothers to me. One of them actually was my brother—Damon—and the others were like adopted brothers. I was ready to go the distance with those guys.

Then? It all just went away. I will unpack the details of how that played out later, but for now, I'll just say there was a betrayal. And it was a deal breaker. The music we'd been playing together, the traveling, the shows we had booked all suddenly came to a screeching halt.

I vividly remember exactly how hopeless I felt on that bitter day when my dream had breathed its last dying breath. All the excitement, all the plans, all my aspirations and expectations of what life was supposed to look like—of who I was "supposed" to be—was replaced by silence. Everything I had worked hard to achieve felt like a waste of time. That's not a feeling you ever forget.

Picture me walking to an early-morning class in the cold, with icy pellets tormenting me.

I don't remember anything that happened during that class. I don't even remember which professor I had for that class. I only remember the overwhelming emotion that began tumbling out of me during the walk back to the house I shared with some of the guys. In a daze of despair and confusion, I began to notice that the frozen shards of ice were mingling with hot tears running down my face. Then there was a voice. Not an audible voice, but a clear question began to form in my mind. This had happened before, and I understood it to be the voice of Jesus. The simple question I heard was this: *Do you want to leave, too?*

When I heard that question, I knew exactly what it meant. The night before, I had read in my Bible the story of Jesus asking his twelve disciples this same question. The context of his question in John 6 is that his disciples were experiencing the death of a dream, too. Jesus's ministry had been growing. Crowds of people had come to hear him speak, and he had been doing miracles. In fact, he had just fed thousands of people with a few fish and a couple loaves of bread. That small lunch donated by a little boy had miraculously fed thousands, and everyone marveled about it. The disciples' dreams seem to have been wrapped up in who they wanted Jesus to be and maybe what they wanted Jesus to do for them. They probably thought the prestige, power, and popularity of Jesus would bring good things their way.

As long as Jesus kept doing miracles and gaining followers, they were all on board. When he spoke of "the Kingdom," they would have naturally imagined he was planning to overthrow the Roman government and put them in positions of power. But in John 6, Jesus revealed some dream-shattering things. He even foretold his own death, explaining how his death and resurrection would pave the way for humanity to experience God in ways they'd never known.

He uses a metaphor, telling them they would drink his blood and eat his flesh to remember him, but all they heard was "cannibalism." So that was weird. Talk about confusing.

As the story goes, droves of followers deserted Jesus, undoubtedly feeling betrayed by what they were hearing. Nothing was working out the way they thought it would. As more and more people started to distance themselves from Jesus, he turned to his twelve closest confidants and asked them, "Are you going to leave, too?"

That was the question ringing in my head and breaking my heart on the day when everything came crashing down. I knew the answer I was supposed to give. But I was so disappointed with God. I felt like I had no choice. The life I thought I was going to live, the potential I thought I had, the dreams that filled me with meaning, passion, and drive—it was all gone.

The space where that dream had taken up residence inside me was suddenly vacated. In its place was only despair rattling around inside me. Even still, I felt as if Jesus was giving me a choice. Looking back, it was more than a choice. It was an invitation.

In the story, Simon Peter spoke up and asked, "To whom would we go?"

Sure, I knew that was Peter's answer. But behind those words, I could almost feel the inner chill he must have felt. He knew Jesus, and he believed in him, yet, in that moment, his feelings didn't match up. Peter chose faith in the Jesus he knew over his feelings about how things appeared in that moment.

I knew I had the option to die with my dream. Or I could accept the invitation to see what life Jesus might be creating. At the end of that cold day in January 2000, through tears and sleet, I mustered up the courage to answer.

"Where else am I going to go?" I uttered under my breath. Like Peter, I chose to believe that Jesus's words held life. That was the moment when I chose faith in what I knew of him over the fear of what I didn't know of the future. I would choose facts over feelings. In that moment I accepted the divine invitation, even though my feelings didn't match up. It was in this moment that the truth of Jesus's words in Matthew 5 became truth for my life, "You're blessed when you feel you've lost what is most dear to you. Only then can you be embraced by the One most dear to you" (Matthew 5:4).

When a dream dies, it's easy to think your story is happening in a vacuum. And when the action adventure suddenly feels more like a horror flick, we can start to believe the dream is unsurvivable. We might imagine the next scene will read "The End" as the credits start to roll.

If you're at a point right now where you're disparaging over a dream you hold dear, remember that this is only a chapter. I wish someone had told me this when I was grieving the loss of my dream. But it's true. When we come to the end of our plan for our story, we're actually being invited into a bigger story.

In your story, you're the main character. So when your micro story feels like it's going off the rails, it's easy to become convinced that whole story is ruined and that God isn't interested or involved. But I happen to believe that couldn't be further from the truth.

Think about the saga of the entire human race as the macro story we are all living in. And throughout the history of the world, every life and every story that ever existed has been woven together in a breathtaking tapestry of joy and pain, heartbreak and healing, highs and lows. Not only are we connected to one another as part of the most epic story, but we are also ultimately connected to the Cosmic Mastermind who is writing it. He invites every one of us to co-create a better story with bigger dreams, visions, and purposes than we ever knew existed.

Whether or not you can see it right now, you have been created on purpose and for a purpose. Your story is far from over. As this chapter comes to a close, know that your greatest chapter may have just begun. Even if nothing makes sense at this moment, just know this: You are exactly where you need to be right now. So keep going. Walk with me through whatever comes next. Let's see what happens. All you need to do is turn the page.

*Chapter Two*

# MY BRO, JOE

You're blessed when you're at the end of your rope. With less of you there is more of God and his rule.

—*Matthew 5:3*

S peaking of epic stories, here's one for you. A guy named Joseph lived thousands of years ago, yet I feel this brotherly connection with him. Like me, he had big dreams and aspirations. Joseph was a dreamer and a visionary. He was ambitious. But he was far from perfect, just like me.

Maybe you'll relate to him, too.

The death of Joseph's dream, like mine, involved betrayal from a band of brothers who happened to be his actual brothers. Instead of crying alone in a sleet storm, the death of Joseph's dream happened in the bottom of a cistern, which is an underground reservoir that stores rainwater. Fortunately for Joseph, there was no water in it at the time. But that dry cistern is where his brothers threw him right before they sold him into slavery. Yes, you read that correctly. His brothers literally sold him to merchants on their way to Egypt, where he would work as a slave indefinitely.

To give you some back story, he had been his dad's favorite son ever since he was born.

That was no secret. He was the youngest of twelve brothers, and Genesis 37:3–4 says: "Israel loved Joseph more than any of his other sons because he was the child of his old age. And he made him an elaborately embroidered coat."

So it was obvious that Joseph was the favorite child, and he even had the technicolor dream coat to prove it. Maybe they didn't have rock bands back then, but if they did, Joseph would have been the front man. The combination of his own ambition and his father, Jacob (also known as Israel), playing favorites, caused him to get a pretty big head. His brothers were not fans, to put it mildly.

I can relate to Joseph's arrogance. When I look back at the less mature, more ambitious version of myself, I kind of want to punch myself in the face. God was kinder than I am to the younger me.

Arrogance can become especially problematic when we are pursuing a dream we believe is from God…or at least for God. It seems like whenever we hitch our ambition wagons to "God's purposes" or try to fill our "significance suitcases" with work we believe God gave us to do, it's easy to get self-righteous. That's where I was before my dream died. And that's where Joseph found himself.

With all those family dynamics going on, Joseph had a pretty crazy dream, which he shared with his brothers. He was like, "Listen to this dream I had. We were all out in the field gathering bundles of wheat, when suddenly my bundle stood straight up and your bundles circled around it and bowed down to mine."

Needless to say, this announcement did nothing to strengthen Joseph's relationship with his brothers. They resented him even more after learning about his dream. It wasn't bad enough that he was spoiled and arrogant, but now he was dreaming about lording over them?

Soon Joseph had another dream. Of course he wasted no time telling his father and his brothers about this dream, too, because some people just don't know how to keep their mouths shut. In this second dream, the sun, the moon, and eleven stars bowed down to him. The stars represented his eleven brothers, and the sun and moon represented his parents.

After he explained the dream to his father and brothers, his father reprimanded him. I can only imagine how that conversation went. "Dude. Seriously? You're making this really awkward."

Now the brothers were really furious. Their hatred for him was worse than ever, and his father agonized over the whole situation.

At this point, Joseph was seeing his future from the perspective of his own micro story. He had no idea how his family's story fit into the bigger story, which was about more than just Joseph's success, authority, or happiness.

God would eventually write a story of redemption, reconciliation, and resurrection, not just for Joseph, but for his family and his country. The ripple effect of his story would impact the world for generations. Joseph had an essential role to play, which was cool. What wasn't so cool is all the pain he would go through before his life's purpose was fully realized.

One day, some of Joseph's brothers went out to pasture their father's sheep. After they had been out for a while, Jacob asked Joseph to go check on them to see how they were doing. He was instructed to report back to Jacob. So Joseph set off to check on the brothers, just as his father asked. When the brothers spotted him coming their direction, they quickly cooked up a plot to kill him.

"Here comes that dreamer! Let's kill him and throw him into one of these old cisterns," they conspired. "We can tell Dad that a vicious animal attacked him and ate him! We'll see what his dreams amount to then!" I imagine somewhere in there was probably a villainous "Muaa-haa-haaa!"

Then one of the brothers, Reuben, intervened with a slightly more level head and said, "No murder. We're not going to kill him. Let's just throw him in the cistern out here in the wild."

Apparently Reuben convinced the other brothers that nature would take its course and they wouldn't actually need to kill him to get rid of him. Reuben secretly planned to go back later, get Joseph out, and take him back to his father. So Reuben went back home and left Joseph in the hands of the brothers until he could return.

When Joseph reached his brothers, they ripped off the colorful coat their father had given him and threw him in the cistern. Then they sat down to eat, like nothing had ever happened.

In the distance, they saw a caravan of Ishmaelites approaching on their way from Delia. Their camels were loaded with spices, ornaments, and perfumes, indicating that they must be on their way to Egypt with goods they were planning to sell at the market there.

In that moment, one of the brothers had an idea. Judah asked his brothers what they would gain by killing their brother and concealing the evidence. Why not sell him to the Ishmaelites who were headed their way? Then they could get rid of him without leaving him as prey for wild animals, and they would even get some money out of the deal. The brothers agreed.

By that time, the traders were approaching the brothers, who pulled Joseph out of the cistern and sold him for twenty pieces of silver to the Ishmaelites. Instead of crying in a sleet storm like I did, Joseph was held captive on a wagon headed for Egypt, where he would be far from the love and admiration he was used to receiving from his father.

Later, his brother Reuben came back to rescue Joseph from the cistern. When he got there…no Joseph. The other brothers hadn't clued him in on what they'd done. Naturally, Reuben assumed Joseph had actually been eaten by wild animals and he ripped his clothes, which was a customary act of mourning.

"The boy is gone! What am I going to do?" Reuben pleaded with his brothers.

Being the jerks they were, they had butchered a goat, dipped Joseph's coat in the blood, and took his coat back to their father, pretending to wonder if this was Joseph's coat.

Jacob recognized the coat at once, of course. In that moment his own dreams—all the hopes and plans he had for his son—were destroyed. All he could do was imagine Joseph being torn limb from limb by a wild animal. Jacob then tore his clothes and dressed in burlap, signifying his inconsolable grief. His sons and daughters tried to comfort him, but he refused their comfort.

Can you imagine how badly Joseph's life seemed to be running off the tracks at that point? The confusion, the pain, the despair, the betrayal of his own brothers...Where was God?

He thought God had given him the dreams he had for his life. This wasn't how it was supposed to end! But it wasn't the end. It was just a chapter.

God's plans for Joseph were really big, and really good, but first he got a major helping of humble pie. In my experience, we either choose to humble ourselves or life has a way of humiliating us. It's a guarantee. Trust me on this. Or at least trust Jesus's words in our next beatitude: "You're blessed when you're at the end of your rope. With less of you there is more of God and his rule" (Matthew 5:3).

I would discover, over time, that God doesn't actually humble us. Humbling ourselves is a choice only we can make. Anyone who concludes that God is a bully who inflicts pain on us for not falling in line with his plans has misunderstood the point—and misunderstood the Father's amazing love for us. We invite the experience of humiliation into our own lives when we are habitually arrogant. We really do reap what we sow. That is a reality we cannot get around.

Save yourself some trouble and choose humility rather than trying to work around it. I've already tried all the ways to get out of it, and they weren't worth it. So did Joseph.

The upshot of facing failure and disappointment is the opportunity that we are continually given to choose humility. When we are humble and honest, we are more able to see that our story isn't actually about us.

Pride and arrogance are not our friends. They will always get in the way of our dreams rather than help us fulfill them. When it comes to life wisdom, the book of Proverbs is full of it, and it also has a lot to say about pride. Proverbs 2:11 says that pride leads only to shame. Proverbs 8:13 tells us pride and arrogance are the way of evil speech. Proverbs 18:12 warns that before destruction, a man's heart is arrogant.

God is inclined to offer mercy to those who choose humility. This truth is woven throughout the stories of the Bible. James 4:6 in The Passion Translation says, "He continues to pour out more and more grace upon us, for God resists you when you are proud, but continually pours out grace when you are humble."

These reminders and Joseph's story confirm what I have personally experienced. Our most humbling experiences open the door to grace. Not just grace as in forgiveness, but grace that God is with us and walking us through the darkest valleys. Humility opens the door to grace, then grace invites us into a deeper life that moves in harmony with the dreams God has for us and for the world.

Later in Joseph's story, others in his life would betray him, too. But even when everyone betrayed and abandoned Joseph, he learned how to become completely dependent on God. The invitation had been there all along, but he had to accept it and act on it. I wonder if the death of Joseph's dream forced him to face the question Jesus asked the disciples—the same question I faced when my dream fell apart: "Will you leave, too?"

Maybe you're having your own "Will you leave?" moment right now. Or maybe your bags are packed and you're on a midnight train headed anywhere God isn't. Maybe your answer to that question is "Yep. I definitely want to leave, too. Peace out."

In those moments when the micro story is all you can see and everything feels terrible, remember the macro story. Something bigger is always happening, always inviting you in. There is always more to your story than what you see. It's hard to believe this when your dream isn't turning out the way you imagined it, but if your version of the dream is truly the best thing for you and for the world, God wouldn't withhold it for anything.

Maybe, like Joseph, you find yourself fighting for a micro dream that's mostly about you.

Maybe the waiting is actually preparing you for something much better than you have the capacity to carry right now. Maybe your dream is the biggest one you can imagine, but what if that dream is way too small? Trust me, and my bro, Joe: It probably is.

## Chapter Three
# BIRTH OF THE DREAM

I f you ever feel crazy because your dream won't leave you alone, just know that it's there for good reasons. Whether your dream is about a career, a family, a relationship, or making an impact on the world, you didn't plant those longings into yourself. You were born with them.

There is something built into the DNA of every human being that tells us there is more to life—more to us—than what we can see in the mirror. We are more than our physical bodies, more than our beliefs about ourselves, and more than others' opinions of us.

We've been designed with souls that compel us to live meaningful lives. This longing has been there as long as we can remember. Sometimes we can't put our finger on the feeling that pulses through our veins and compels us to keep trying...but we want more of it. We wake up, we feel it. We go to bed at night, we feel it. We just know we need to live lives that make us come alive. When we're not doing that, we might even feel like a part of us is dying.

This book is not just about my dreams and yours. It's also about God's dreams. Before any of us can see our dreams come to fruition, we need to be aware that it isn't just our dream. The roots of our dreams are completely intertwined with the most epic dreams ever…because God has dreams, too.

Maybe it seems weird to think about God having dreams, but the genius expressed in the natural world—and in us—serves as a constant reminder that our dreams originate in the heart and mind of a loving Creator. The idea that we are "created in his image" is another way of understanding that our very existence is directly tied to the same love and value woven like a golden thread through every fiber of creation. And though his dreams for us may involve work he has planned for us, his dream includes walking with us just as he longed to walk with Adam and Eve through the garden for the sheer enjoyment.

God dreamed you up. He imagined the world with you in it, and here you are. Let that sink in for a moment. You started as a dream in the heart and the mind of God. His dream started long before you were born and will continue long after your last breath. Everything that exists in our universe began in the imagination of God. We are his dreams come true.

There is no other creation like human beings. God created all the heavens and the earth and all the animals and the plants and the trees. And he said it was all good. Yet none of creation has been made in his image like humanity. We have been invited to join him in the creative endeavor of bringing dreams to life.

The reality is, if we're created in his image, that means the emotions we experience in the process of creating dreams for the future started first in his heart. That means he understands how we feel because he has experienced those emotions before we did.

We are like him in many ways. So we dream, we create, and we live within a reality that was once just an idea which he turned it into reality. Maybe this is why creating your dreams brings such amazing joy. God knows this joy.

Our dreams offer us a tiny glimpse of the greatness born into us that goes far beyond ourselves. Genesis describes how God created all that there is, and even now I'm blown away by the idea that the "otherness" embedded in our DNA brings with it a sense of awe and purpose.

This makes sense when we think about how tapping into our creativity can be a deeply spiritual experience. Creativity never stops crying out for expression. All the stories I grew up hearing make more sense when I think of how God birthed a universe he was passionate about and planted in us the seeds of dreams that would make the universe more complete and ultimately more connected to the macro story of his divine, eternal dream.

I can't imagine the joy God must have felt as he created the universe. We get a taste of that joy when we create, too. Think of your earliest memories creating as a kid. Do you remember building sandcastles or turning cardboard boxes into forts? Do you remember feeling compelled to draw pictures of the things you loved? Or singing songs at the top of your lungs without fear, just because it felt good? For me, as a kid, it wasn't hard to understand the joy of creating. As an adult it was so comforting to understand that our heavenly Father shares our joy when co-creating with us. A mentor of mine once said, "If you're excited about doing something with God, remember that he's ten times more excited than you are." I think that is true.

As we get older and life happens, things can get a bit more complicated. We might get busy with life and forget to find creative expression. Or we get more self-conscious or perfectionistic about it. Hopefully you still allow yourself to experience the unadulterated joy of creating. Because that need to create is born into every one of us because God's divine nature is built into each of us. Whether we are creating companies, ministries, or solutions to problems, we are born to create. Those of us with children, too, understand the joy of co-creating with God when we see the miracle of life that we're part of. God knows that joy, because he experienced it when we came into the world.

The early seeds of our dreams are lovingly planted in us when we are too young to understand it. When I think about the seedling stage of my dream, after Stryper inspired me to be a drummer, I better understand how the longing to create was so unstoppable. It wasn't just the fact that Stryper was legit enough to be on MTV and secular radio, or that their neon bumblebee- colored album cover captured my impressionable attention. It was that my need to connect with something big and meaningful—that longing to be part of something significant—was embedded into my DNA by design. The joy of creating music and life-changing experiences made me feel connected to people, to myself, and to the God who loves to create. I fully believe God invites every single one of us to co-create with him in some way.

What starts as a seed has potential to grow and flourish long before it grows into anything. Every seed is packed with potential that takes time and attention to fully realize. But as we grow and nurture it, we get glimpses of God's dream for how the universe is made to operate and where we fit into it. As our understanding evolves, our roots deepen, and growth happens, we are able to see more fully what we couldn't quite grasp when all we could see was a tiny seed.

Years later, I would come to understand more about how God weaves into us a certain spiritual DNA. But as a kid, all I knew was how happy and alive I felt whenever I was drumming. Or talking about drumming. Or drawing stage plans on the blank side of offering envelopes during my dad's sermons... or going to concerts where other people were creating the kinds of experiences I wanted to create someday. I studied secular artists who had huge followings, and I took mental notes on how I could grow into the kind of artist who could literally rock someone's world.

When I look back with the perspective I didn't have then, it's not surprising that I was obsessed with learning and growing as a musician. Everything in my life was focused on drumming because, somewhere way down deep, creating brought joy and fulfillment that pushed me in the direction I needed to go. It woke up the gifts inside me that would be important for the rest of my life.

As I reminisce about the first inklings of my dream in those early years, I invite you to think back to when yours took root, too. Whatever you were dreaming about as a kid was the start of something significant. It may not have made sense for many years. It still may not make sense. But something important was forming in you that deserves to be honored. I fully believe that thing, whatever it is, can be traced all the way back to the imagination of God. So give that young dreamer some mad respect.

The third grade version of my dream felt as serious as the adult version of my dream does now. After my third grade year, my dad's job took our family to Phoenix, Arizona. My new school in Phoenix had a band program for fourth graders, so I signed up to be a drummer in the fourth grade band.

I. Was. Stoked.

I would soon learn, however, that kids who join the fourth grade band are not immediately endowed with a full drum kit. They get a snare drum. One little snare drum. That's it. So lame. But that's how an elementary school drummer gets to begin. So I was signed up and ready for my snare drum to arrive. At last, I could start pursuing my destiny.

That summer, however, we moved again. This time, we moved to Tempe, Arizona, where the school district did not have a band program for fourth grade students. Band started in the fifth grade there. I was heartbroken. I would like to tell you I waited patiently for that year to pass, but in eleven-year-old time, it felt like a decade.

My fifth grade year eventually arrived and, when it did, a school-issued snare drum was finally mine. I brought it home and unpacked it like it was the Holy Grail. I carefully set up the drum, sat down, and got ready for my triumphant moment. I'd been thinking about this moment for well over a year and had a lot of time to prepare. I had already decided which song I would play first. It was a tough call, but I was confident in my choice.

I would play the drum fill from Poison's "Fallen Angel." If you know the song, you know the drum fill.

Alone in my bedroom, with no one listening, I made my drumming debut playing that snare fill. Boy, did I play the heck out of that fill. It was on.

Many years later, while attending a Poison concert, I snuck backstage. Turns out, I'm really good at that. If we hang out sometime, ask me about the time the security guard at a Mötley Crüe concert almost killed me. I didn't end up in a cistern like Joseph, but I now appreciate how quickly things can escalate.

Anyway, I snuck backstage and struck up a conversation with Rikki Rockett, the drummer for Poison. I told him that the first thing I ever played as a drummer was that fill from "Fallen Angel." He laughed and thought it was awesome. Then he told me what inspired him to play that fill. To be honest, I don't even remember what he said. Maybe I was too stunned to be talking to Rikki Rockett that I couldn't actually focus on what he was saying. But, regardless of what inspired him, he had inspired me when my dream was still coming to life, and I was glad I got to tell him that and say thank you.

I was a quick study on the drums. I was highly motivated, and holding down the rhythm came naturally to me. God had seemingly embedded a natural ability for percussion into my DNA. I even made honor band during the summer after sixth grade.

That year I also got my first full drum set. My brother, Damon, got his first guitar as an eighth grade graduation present that same year. These gifts communicated to us that our parents saw something in us, too. I can now better appreciate what a sacrifice it might have been for them to give me such a loud instrument. I'm grateful they did. Our church in Tempe was the perfect place to rehearse. I'm sure Mom and Dad agreed because it wasn't at home. We spent hours and hours for years and years rehearsing on the empty church platform.

Up to that point, we hadn't found anybody to join our rock and roll dream. So it was just the two of us honing our craft together, until one high school English presentation turned into a golden opportunity for our first public performance in the school theater. My buddy Mike had started learning to play bass so we recruited him. Then we convinced our other buddy Bobby that he could sing. He couldn't, but his stage energy almost made up for his lack of singing talent.

I commandeered this English presentation on the topic of hearing loss as our stage debut.

With Mike on bass, Bobby on vocals, Damon on guitar, and me on drums, we started with "Eruption" by Van Halen. Damon nailed Eddie Van Halen's guitar solo, then we went into their cover of "You Really Got Me," which we had timed to a full light show. I suspect that project on hearing loss potentially caused hearing loss for a few of the teachers, but I know for sure that it was one of the greatest moments of my life up to that point. I followed up the performance with a persuasive speech about hearing loss, and I'd never been more excited about an English assignment.

That experience only fanned the flames of my dream. I could not unfeel the way I came alive when I was doing what I loved to do. From then on, Damon and I started playing every time we got a chance.

I was fortunate that growing up as a pastor's kid was a good experience for me. A lot of pastors' kids I know now have had difficult experiences, so I'm grateful for my parents. They were consistent and authentic. I didn't see one version of my dad preaching on Sundays and a completely different version on Tuesdays. He was always the same. My parents weren't perfect, but they did not pretend to be. They modeled their lives after Jesus and gave Damon and me a solid foundation at home. I will always be grateful that they supported us, even if they didn't fully understand our obsession with neon spandex, long hair, or rock and roll.

I watched my dad's life closely, and there was a lot to admire. He was a good man. Like most kids, I also began to study the lives of other heroes of mine, like Tommy Lee, founding member and drummer for Mötley Crüe. He also had a life I admired for completely different reasons. I was pretty sure my dad wasn't rich, and he definitely didn't drive cool sports cars.

Tommy Lee, on the other hand, seemed to have money coming out of his ears and had tons of cool cars. He also had a lot girlfriends, and clearly God was keeping my dad to one woman. Of course, I'm grateful he stayed with my mom for life. That, too, is a rare gift they gave us. But, as grateful as I was for grounded, consistent parents, I was nervous that God was going to keep me from having an exciting, Tommy Lee–level life.

My fears were reinforced when missionaries came to speak at our church. They talked about following God's dream for their lives, yet from what I could tell he'd sent them halfway across the world to eat weird food and wear clothing Tommy Lee wouldn't be caught dead wearing. Instead of black and neon spandex, like Stryper, the missionaries all showed up in the same four-pocket khaki shirt. I swear that shirt must've been standard issue in missionary boot camp. Inevitably, at some point during their visit, I would hear about their most recent encounter with an anaconda or see a giant snakeskin displayed on their table of memorabilia in the church lobby and think, *How could a loving God send them into the jungle in that shirt to eat gross food and live among deadly snakes?* I didn't know, but I was pretty sure if the mission field was what he had in mind for me, instead of music, that's how it would all end for me—devoured by snakes and survived only by that terrible khaki shirt.

I wanted to have an awesome life and be the kind of man God was proud of. I wasn't trying to achieve this dream apart from him. I wanted to do it with him. I just hoped maybe he would consider that detail and pull a few strings for me not to end up in a story that didn't feel like me. Surely, if he knew me at all, God would smile on me for being a good guy like my dad while also letting me live a big, bold adventure I could get excited about. So, with that in mind, I went for it, full steam ahead.

## Chapter Four

# GET YOUR YOKE ON

One of the challenges of our church in Tempe was that it was tiny and there weren't many teenagers at our church. Often youth gatherings consisted only of my brother, me, and an adult leader. If I was going to live a Tommy Lee–level life, I needed to get out and meet some people.

For that reason and a few others, I lived for church camp every summer. For one week every year, my brother and I traveled to the mountains of Prescott, Arizona, where we got to spend the week with kids our age from other churches around Arizona. That experience became the highlight of every summer.

During high school, I was invited to play drums for the worship band during camp. This was great, because it combined so many things I loved: camp, playing drums, and my growing understanding of God. I also don't mind admitting that there were a lot of cute girls at camp who were at least somewhat cool with Jesus. So, I ask you, what's not to love about getting all those things rolled into one glorious week every year?

Those summer camp experiences became like steroids for me spiritually. Summer camp of 1993, in particular, changed my life forever. The camp speaker that year was Jimmy Johnson. He had pastored in California, where I assumed all the coolest people came from, and Jimmy was larger than life in my eyes. He was a tall, energetic, unapologetic follower of Jesus with a big, booming voice that never sounded boring.

Jimmy was always telling us, "Get your yoke on!" Which might sound like a weird thing to say. But he was quoting Jesus, who said, "Come to me, all of you who are weary and carry heavy burdens, and I will give you rest. Take my yoke upon you. Let me teach you, because I am humble and gentle at heart, and you will find rest for your souls. For my yoke is easy to bear, and the burden I give you is light" (Matthew 11:28–30 NLT). That verse was one I would come back to at many important points in my life.

We don't hear much about yokes these days, but before plows and tractors, yokes were a necessity of life for people to grow food, move heavy things, and pull wagons of people from place to place. A yoke kept animals moving in the same direction so the work could be done more easily and effectively using their combined strength.

When Jesus walked the earth, he was a master carpenter in a Jewish family. Jewish tradition suggests that he was likely known in his community for hand-carving yokes to perfectly fit his neighbors' animals. This metaphor Jesus shares clearly comes out of his deep knowledge and love for every living thing.

He understood, better than most, how to create a yoke that felt right and supported essential work rather than hindering it.

Jesus reveals, through this analogy, that we are created to be divinely supported in ways that make our life's work less burdensome and more impactful. Being yoked with him is not some generic, one-size-fits-all situation. It is a picture of how Jesus invites us to bring our unique strengths and dreams into alignment with his. As a result of being yoked with him, metaphorically, we're not constantly pulling and tugging in opposition to the person we're created to be. We were never meant to work with an ill-fitting burden intended to hold us down or control us.

What a relief it was to learn that being yoked with Christ creates a life of eternal connection to his love, support, and understanding. It wasn't a heavy, counterproductive burden. Mine was designed to fit me like spandex, not khaki canvas! That was an important thing for me to hear from Jimmy Johnson on that summer night in 1993. I had been so afraid my life was going to suck if I entrusted my dreams to God. Rather, I was finally beginning to understand that his dreams and mine were two sides of the same coin.

We don't have to find our purpose in a vacuum or do our work in solitude, with our own limited strength. We just need to trust enough to keep our part of the deal and let him do the lion's share of the work alongside us. We show up and work in cooperation with the One who knows us, loves us, and wants nothing more than to see us become all we're uniquely created to be.

Jimmy's challenge for us at that week was to get our head in the yoke and not try to fight against the help God wants to offer.

The problem is, most of us have trouble getting our head into that space. I know I did.

I'll never forget that night Jimmy preached this sermon. I can see it right now. I was sitting about three-fourths of the way back on the left side of the room. At the end of the service, he asked if anybody sensed that God was calling them to full-time Christian ministry. I got up and went down to the front of the church, overwhelmed with emotion, humility, and gratitude that God would invite me to walk and to work with him. I remember kneeling down next to other kids who had also come forward. We felt the hands of our leaders behind us praying for us.

That moment changed the trajectory of my life. As I look back on that night, one observation breaks my heart, though. The majority of kids didn't feel called in those moments, so they didn't get prayed for. They didn't get hugged and high-fived. They weren't celebrated.

What I now know to be true is that every single person in that room was called by God to accept the light, supportive, custom-created yoke that was created for them by the Master Creator. For generations, well-meaning people have taught kids (and adults, too, for that matter) that some people are called and everyone else is on their own. I wish I could go back to that night on that mountain in Prescott, look every one of those students in the eyes, and say, "Every single one of you are called to God's dreams. Whether your dream is full-time ministry or not, God has unique dreams that are tailored just for you. No matter what path you choose for your career, you have the potential to change the world."

Right now, wherever you are, imagine me high-fiving you, celebrating your gifts, praying for you, and cheering you on in your dreams. Then imagine Jesus right there next to you, sharing the work and giving you the assurance that you were never expected to pull off your dream alone. No one is more excited than he is about the custom-designed adventure he has been working on for you since the dawn of time.

We're all invited into the grand adventure. You are not a spectator here. You're invited to fully participate—to get your yoke on. It is an invitation to love and be loved. It involves the qualities born into you that bring light and love into the world. It's not meant to exclude, but to include and support.

Whether or not you grew up in church like I did, it's easy to mistake Jesus's invitation as an invitation to church. But Jesus, didn't say, "Hey, if you're weary and heavy-laden…come to church." The invitation is to Jesus. He isn't hard to find when we're looking. And we don't have to walk into a church to let him guide our decisions.

Getting your yoke on is about inviting divine support—simply because he loves you. I fully believe God wants your dreams to happen more than you do, which I know may seem impossible. He gives us an example to follow, along with stories and challenges that help us understand how to live God's dream while also being human. He knows what it's like to walk through life on an imperfect planet.

When life gets complicated or we lose our way, it's easy to forget that he has never once lost sight of us. He isn't waiting at the end of some imaginary finish line out in the future to see how we finish; he is right in the middle of all the blood, sweat, and tears, grinding it out with us here and now.

Ephesians 2:10 (NLT) says that we are "God's masterpiece. He has created us anew in Christ Jesus, so we can do the good things he planned for us long ago."

He has always intended for us to walk alongside Christ through the ups and the downs and everything in between. I can say now that there's no doubt God was cheering me on during the greatest moments and weeping with me in moments I didn't think I could survive. If he did that for me, he is doing it for you, too, right this very moment.

*Chapter Five*

# INDIANA

It was easy to accept the invitation to *get* my yoke on, but it was much more difficult over the next few years to *keep* it on. Like Joseph, I kept trying to make my dream happen my own way and using my own wisdom—or lack thereof. Even though I believed in Jesus and genuinely wanted to make him proud, I found it nearly impossible to release the death grip I had on my dream. As much as I wanted to believe I had surrendered it fully to God, I still didn't truly trust him with it. I didn't *really* believe God wasn't going to make my life suck in order to test my commitment.

At that point, most everything you needed to know about me was summed up in the musical stew of all of my favorite bands. Van Halen, U2, Guns N' Roses, Mötley Crüe, Metallica, Extreme, and Stryper—those were the bands whose songs explained my whole deal, the good and the bad. On a good day, I might be more like Robert Sweet or Bono. On a bad day, I'd probably be more like Tommy Lee.

When it came time to choose a college, I settled on a college in Indiana. Knowing full well that my college destination wasn't exactly known for warmth and sunshine, I hoped that small act of surrender might at least earn a nod from God. I wasn't wearing a khaki four-pocket shirt in Sri Lanka, but surely he could see that I was willing to do hard things—like enduring Indiana winters—for the sake of my calling.

I remember so clearly the first night I left home to drive to Indiana. The old 1966 pickup truck my dad had bought us—and helped us restore with the help of some primer gray spray paint—had until that point been an Arizona truck. By that, I mean it had never spent a single moment in a Midwest winter situation, where the mix of ice and salt would cause the inevitable rust-out that happens to Indiana trucks. My dad had his associate's degree in auto mechanics and did some mechanic work through the years, but I'm not entirely sure whether or not he fully knew how to restore a twenty-year-old truck. We thought the truck was pretty cool, though, and it definitely was the only one of its kind.

In order to drive it from Arizona to Indiana, Dad knew we would need to put all of our stuff in the back of the truck, so we needed a camper shell. There was one problem. No one was making camper shells that matched 1966 trucks. So the one that my dad found and installed didn't quite fit. It extended above the cab a good six inches. It was a horrendous sight.

It took about an hour for Damon and me to load up everything we owned into the back of the truck. There was my drum set, a couple of suitcases of clothes, the brand new three-disc CD boombox I had received as a graduation present, Damon's 4×12

5150 Eddie van Halen amp head and cabinet, his guitars, stereo, and a couple more suitcases of his clothes.

When I realized everything I owned was in the back of that pickup truck and life as I knew it was in the rearview mirror, the reality hit me pretty hard. Moving across the country for a vision that I felt I was called to create suddenly felt terrifying. All the passion in the world didn't take away the fear of the unknown.

I remember pulling into Albuquerque, New Mexico, after about eight solid hours of driving, to rest for the night. We were far from home and not even close to our destination. I was leaving my mom and my dad, all my best friends, the city and state I loved…and I was probably never coming back. So I did what anyone would do. I laid my head on the pillow of that Albuquerque hotel and wept, trying my best to stifle the sobs so my brother didn't know I was crying. Looking back, I supposed maybe he was crying, too.

We drove, and drove, and drove until we finally rolled into that small town in Indiana in our primer-gray makeshift camper, looking like Arizona hillbillies.

Not long after arriving in Indiana, I was asked to help lead worship for a local church's youth group and was astonished to learn that there was a hot debate going on about whether or not the church would allow drums on the platform. Apparently our churches in Arizona were using a different playbook than the state of Indiana. Their church board had to take a vote on it.

In my mind, this was unfathomable. I mean, not only should the drums be on the platform, but they should be on a drum riser, supported by a large cage of trussing with lights all around it, and it should elevate above the stage and rotate 360 degrees while the drummer is playing. And we're questioning whether or not drums should be on the platform at all? Yikes.

It was at this point in my life when I began to learn that my vision wouldn't be understood or appreciated by some people. I learned not to be surprised or disheartened if I could see ideas or possibilities others couldn't see yet. Maybe that's why I relate to Joseph, who had dreams about his future no one could understand or get behind for years. Sometimes, when we have a vision for the way things could be, there are people who just aren't ready for it.

I believed music could bridge the gap between people who follow Jesus and people who don't give a rip about Jesus. It was a way to bring people together and connect awesome music with a love that is bigger than any of us. And as the years went by, this theme would be recurring: bringing people together and making sure they know they are loved and valued, not just by me but by the Creator of the universe.

During my freshman year of college, you'll never believe who came to speak. Just as I was grappling with how to keep my dream alive in a place that I wasn't too excited about, in walked Jimmy Johnson, whom I hadn't seen since that life-changing week at camp where I first got my yoke on.

I was reminded to keep that yoke on in the powerful and loving words of this gentle giant of a man. Sadly, that would be the last time I ever heard him speak. Jimmy died a few years after that. I am still so grateful for the impact his words and life had on me at two important crossroads in my life. I imagine the welcome parade that must have happened for him on the other side. He taught so many people to live lovingly and unapologetically, and he exemplified those things in the way he lived his life.

In Jimmy's memory, his family created silver replicas of the wooden yoke necklace he always wore. I bought one, of course. Then I bought some to give as gifts to my groomsmen the day I got married. A few years later I got a tattoo of that yoke on my arm. And, many years later, when my oldest son turned sixteen, I gave him my original yolk necklace. So to say the idea of being yoked with Christ has changed my life would be an understatement.

That first year of college I held tightly to my dream, waiting for the right opportunity to set it into motion, and played for youth groups and chapel services whenever I got the chance. I made it to my sophomore year of college and managed to have no money, no friends, no girlfriend, and no band.

One evening, Damon and I sat in the living room of our terrible apartment, strategizing about what to do. It was there that Damon said something that proved to be wise, as he often did: "Daron, maybe we need to stop trying to do it our way. Maybe we just need to tell God we will use our gifts and abilities in any way he allows us to use them."

That night we prayed together and told God we were here to serve him. We promised to take whatever an opportunity he brought our away. And I'd like to take this opportunity to express in the strongest possible terms: Be careful what you pray for.

Not more than a week after promising God we would stay open to whatever he brought our way, we heard a knock at our door. Apparently, after Damon led worship for a chapel service earlier that day, his guitar hadn't made it into the back of the truck. Outside our door stood two guys I barely knew with

Damon's guitar. The guys were in a singing group on campus, which sang Southern gospel quartet music. They also apparently had a thing for preppy clothing, which is just short of a four-pocket missionary shirt in my mind. Their vibe was everything I didn't want to be, and their music was not my jam.

When they arrived at our door that day, they were excited to deliver Damon's guitar because they had been looking for an opportunity to invite the Earlewine brothers to join their Southern gospel quartet. I couldn't believe my ears. They wanted us to join their preppy Southern gospel group.

They wanted to start leading worship at camps that summer, which they had apparently tried to do a year earlier, but none of them knew how to play instruments. This year they thought they would up the ante and recruit musicians. They explained that we would play some church gigs throughout the semester, then go on tour to camps and churches all summer long.

Once they said the words *go on tour*, I was locked in. I basically didn't hear anything else they said after that. They were going on tour, they wanted us to play for them, and we would be performing for thousands of kids that summer. My brother, always so rational, was not quite so enthused.

After about a month, I finally convinced Damon to do this with me, and we began filling out forms and reading packets of information about joining this group for the summer.

That's when we learned that musicians who traveled for the university were held to strict dress code policies. This was terrible news, because Damon and I had been successfully growing our hair out for over a year and at that point I think I had three earrings. We were just starting to look like rock stars, and now we would have to cut our hair, take out the earrings, and go shopping for khaki pants and dress shirts.

It was at this point we knew with a high level of certainty that God has one raging sense of humor. Years and years of honing our skills and looking for an opportunity to make awesome music that would make him proud and bring people together…and now we're packing khakis and dress shirts for our first summer tour.

"Lord, I've been trying to become the next Robert Sweet or Tommy Lee since third grade, and you're going to make me go on tour looking like a quartet singer?!"

I was super annoyed when, the day I got my hair cut, girls to whom I seemed invisible with my long hair just a day earlier suddenly began to come out of the woodwork to talk to me all across campus. I can't even express to you how unfathomable this was to me. Dudes with long hair are cool. I don't care what you say.

Long story short, we compromised. By the time our midsummer concerts began, we had totally hijacked the Southern gospel show and replaced it with a rock show, but the guys would still sing a short acoustic set at intermission. That was the compromise. Cut the hair, hijack the set.

So off we went to tour for the first time ever. I think we drove thirty thousand miles during the month of May alone. We crisscrossed America that summer playing camps for kids just like the ones I loved so much a few years earlier. We made it all the way to California. The kids at the youth camps loved the music, and we had a blast.

I recorded the name and contact information for every youth camp and venue we played that summer, knowing I had plans to contact them when I had a band of my own.

While in California, we paid a visit to the famous Sunset Strip in Los Angeles and made a point of stopping in front of a famous club called Whisky A Go Go, which I knew of because most of my favorite bands got their start there. Mötley Crüe, Guns N' Roses, Stryper, Van Halen, and other legendary acts had played the Whisky during their rise to rock and roll fame.

Damon and I took a moment, standing outside the Whisky, to let ourselves dream. "A year from today, the Earlewine brothers will be back!" I proclaimed into a video camera. "We're going to play the Whisky!"

Somewhere in a box in an attic, covered in dust, is probably a video documenting that moment. I wish I could find it. But I don't need the video to remember the passion we felt in that moment and that commitment—to ourselves and to each other—that we were going to make it happen.

Allowing ourselves to reengage with our dream energized us. We decided then and there to keep doing the work. The next fall, at the start of my junior year of college, we officially started a band with the guys we had toured with during the summer and we called ourselves Paradigm. Playing at the Whisky on our way to world domination was the new goal.

## Chapter Six

# GENTLE NUDGES

As we started putting the band together, we knew Damon would play guitar and I would play drums, but we needed a bass player, keyboard player, and the all-important right lead singer. Naturally, we went with the people we knew and had relationships with. Aaron had been our sound engineer during the previous summer tour, but he had been learning to play bass. So he became our bass player. Charlie, one of the singers from the summer group, became our keyboard player. And Josh, another singer from the group, became our lead singer. The move from a gospel quartet to a rock band was a big leap for some of the guys, but we pressed on.

My parents had recently moved from Arizona to Mitchell, Indiana, for a year. So, while I was visiting them that summer, I went to a youth camp in southern Indiana. I'm actually not even sure why I went, but I'm glad I did. The first night I attended the camp, I watched a band from another university lead worship. I knew their lead singer, Lee, *had* to be in our band. The power of his voice was undeniable and so inspiring—almost angelic. He communicated songs with an energy that was captivating.

After the service, I talked to Lee for a while. When I went back later in the week, I had a chance to get to know him a little better and a friendship began to form. At the time, he was attending another university, which he also represented as traveling musician. I wondered if we might have the chance to work together at some point, but the timing wasn't right.

Paradigm started rehearsing together that fall, and things weren't clicking with the lead vocals. Josh was a great singer and phenomenal performer, but we agreed that it wasn't a good fit. He would finish the semester with us, then we would need a new lead singer.

When we knew Josh would be parting ways with the band, I tried calling Lee. That was the pre-cellphone era, when we had to use a landline and leave messages for people on answering machines. I started calling Lee's number a couple times a day, leaving long messages trying to persuade him that he needed to transfer schools and move to Indiana, and join our band.

I didn't hear from him at first. Turns out, Lee's friends didn't want him to move, so they were intercepting messages that came in on the answering machine when Lee wasn't around. My messages were often not delivered and, at times, erased from the answering machine. But I was convinced that Lee was our guy and that our meeting was no coincidence. So I persisted.

Eventually, Lee got my messages, and, long story short, he moved to Indiana after first semester to join the band. By the time he joined us the first week of December, we had written a handful of songs and were ready to rehearse. We changed the band name to Paradigm 5 and we delved into writing more songs together.

During the week between Christmas and New Year's Day we attended a national youth convention in Cincinnati, where we competed in a battle of the bands. We had been Paradigm 5 with Lee on lead vocals for less than thirty days when we won the battle of the bands. That was an amazing experience that showed us not only that we had something special, but that others could see something special in us, too.

We went to work even harder, writing songs and sharpening the ones we had already written. By the end of February, we had recorded our best songs and were gigging every chance we got. We spent the rest of that semester booking a sixty-show tour for the summer that would take us from North Carolina to San Diego, Los Angeles, Sacramento, and all the way back across the States.

The energy of our live shows was infectious. With the kind of showmanship we admired in Van Halen, Mötley Crüe, and Stryper, the bar was set high for the level of performance we wanted to deliver. We were always looking for ways to create the wow factor that would set our shows apart from other bands. I'll never forget one particular on-campus concert, after we discovered that the ceiling tiles of the coffee house could be removed. At the beginning of the show, Lee rappelled down onto the stage through the ceiling. It was epic. Shout-out to the student with rappelling experience who helped us pull off that stunt. You know who you are.

I loved every minute of everything we did as a band. But, as the summer went on, and the shows stacked up one after the next, something was shifting inside me. I fought it at first, but then I had to be honest with myself. I found myself feeling a bit caged in by the drums. I had things to say that I couldn't say from behind the drums.

Since that youth camp several summers earlier, I felt called to a life of service to God, but I also didn't want to be a pastor. I wanted to be a drummer in a rock and roll band of Christians. But at the end of our shows, I felt like something was missing.

In the back of my mind, there was still some concern that God might ruin my life, but I was even more concerned that people might walk away from our shows and miss the entire point of what we were singing about. I wanted to be sure the truth didn't get lost in the bright lights and energetic performances—the truth that God loves each person in the room and is *for* them.

In his book *The Art of Work*, Jeff Goins states, "A vocation or a calling is not something you try. It's someone you become." Playing the drums was a talent—something I *did*. But I would discover that my calling was deeper than talent. I was moved and equipped to speak the truth about who I was becoming and who all of us can become when we know we are loved and valued by the Creator of the universe.

Those promptings, when I was given a message to communicate, weren't aggressive shoves. There was no writing on the wall or loud voice calling out to me in the middle of the night. They were quiet invitations into compassionate curiosity. They were invitations that would eventually reveal the person I was becoming.

Maybe you've sensed this kind of conflict within yourself—those moments, when you're doing what you are gifted at doing, yet still feel like there's more inside you that is being revealed. Author Wayne Jacobsen calls these moments gentle nudges from the Spirit. You don't need to protect the way that you've envisioned your dream, especially when you understand that it originated with God. Let's be honest: You're currently only seeing it through the glass dimly lit. These are often invitations into a deeper understanding of yourself, your calling, and your potential. I encourage you to embrace some compassionate curiosity and move toward those nudges when they happen. You can trust the Author of your dreams, who got you here and can take you anywhere you're meant to go.

As I think back, I don't know why I went to that camp that night. I only know that I sensed a gentle nudge. Following that nudge set off a chain reaction, and suddenly important milestones began to fall into place. In that same way, my life has continued to unfold through a series of gentle nudges that opened doors and shaped every chapter. I can say now that I have no regrets, although, as you are about to learn, that doesn't mean everything went my way from that point on.

When we understand that fear doesn't come from God, that we are given a spirit of power, love, and self-control (2 Timothy 1:17), we begin to embrace the joy of being his children, deeply loved for *who* we are and *where* we are. We can begin each new day with expectancy and say to God, "What's next, Dad?! What new adventure are we stepping into today?"

Each time you feel a gentle nudge, trust it. There is nothing to fear and no need to resist it. Each time you respond with curiosity and trust, you step further into becoming the person you are born to be.

*Chapter Seven*

# THE WHISKY

Have you ever had a moment that you just knew was about to change everything? A moment when everything you've been working toward and waiting for has culminated and your highest hopes are about to come to fruition? I sure did.

Strategically, I'd kept the contact information for every event we played during the previous summer tour with the university so I could book a tour for Paradigm 5 in all those same venues. I remember one of my bandmates, Charlie, finding a magazine that was basically a guide to rock and roll touring. Inside its pages was contact information of every rock club in America. I spent hours upon hours calling these clubs, trying to get us booked at rock and roll bars in between camps, conferences, campus events, and church gigs.

What I didn't realize is how visionary and leadership gifts were developing in me that I would use for the rest of my life. I wanted to play these clubs because Van Halen did, but even more than that, I wanted to take the story of Jesus into every-day spaces and places where people were experiencing real life. I wanted to go into clubs and perform really good music and sing about faith, hope, and love in a way that could translate to people who would never set foot in a church. I didn't know it yet, but the pioneering spirit that was part of my spiritual DNA was driving this dream. It just happened to be covered with the heavy lacquer of ambition and self-promotion.

When I called bars, I would introduce myself as Daron Earlewine from D and C Productions in Indianapolis, Indiana. Recalling Jesus's teaching to be shrewd as snakes and as inno-cent as doves, my best attempt at being shrewd was to pretend D and C Productions was totally a thing. D and C stood for Daron and Charlie and in reality, it didn't exist—legally, anyway. How-ever, it definitely existed in my mind.

Charlie and I did the booking and organizing for the band. And since we did travel to Indianapolis from our college town at least once a week, we went with Indianapolis as our home base. It sounded way more legit to say, "This is Daron from D and C Productions in Indianapolis, Indiana, booking a national touring band called Paradigm 5," than it sounded to say, "Hey, this is Daron from Nowhere, Indiana, and I have a startup band. Can we play at your venue?"

After working through our list for months, the day finally came when I got a yes from the Whisky. I remember hanging up the phone and running around our living room and jumping on the couches in celebration.

We did it. That promise we made on video in front of the Whisky during the previous summer was going to become a reality. Something in me just knew that would be the night when we got signed to a record deal.

We did our summer tour of camps and church events, and rock clubs in between. Then finally, the date arrived when we would play the Whisky. We woke up to a beautiful, sunny day in Southern California. We headed to the Whisky to load our gear in, and then we took some time to walk down Sunset Strip and soak in the whole experience. There was another club called the Roxy down the street, and we saw production trucks sitting outside of Roxy. The marquee said, "Worship on the Rocks." We were intrigued.

We walked in and learned that on this very night, just a few bars down the street from the Whisky, a band would be recording a live worship album. We met the director of the event and explained to him who we were and that we would be playing the Whisky later just up the street.

A crowd began to gather for their concert at the Roxy, and they graciously brought us onstage, in front of a packed bar, and explained that Paradigm 5 would be playing down the street at the Whisky that night. They prayed for us and encouraged everyone to come down to our concert. We could hardly believe it. This felt like a divine gift, which only strengthened my belief in the magnitude of this moment for the band.

We headed back to the Whisky, and as the other bands began to load in, we learned that another band that would be playing before we did was called Paradigm. I was glad we had changed our band name to Paradigm 5, but I was thrilled that their band was doing a showcase for every major record company in LA that night. I was even more convinced that this was a gift from

God, because it meant every major record label would be at the Whisky that night.

The bar began to fill with people and tons of A&R directors, the people who find talent—"artist and repertoire"—for major record companies. (Record labels don't have many A&R people now.) It was hard to miss them when we saw them. They were the ones wearing pullovers or polos with their record company logo embroidered on their chest. So I walked around the bar looking for them, and when I found one I would ask, "So who are you here to see tonight?"

Obviously they would say Paradigm, but then I would say, "Yeah, I'm hearing a lot about Paradigm 5, which plays later on tonight. I guess they're supposed to be really hot." I had no idea whether or not it would work, but I was giving it my best shot.

The bar was getting fuller by the minute, and we knew more people would be showing up once the worship concert let out down the street. Paradigm finished playing, and there was one more band up before we would take the stage. This next band was called Bardot.

So Bardot takes the stage wearing some…we'll call them "creative" costumes involving a whole lot of fishnet material. Imagine the artist Meat Loaf and the main character in *The Rocky Horror Picture Show* had a love child. That was Bardot.

Bardot was not easy on the eyes, by any standards, and the band was awful. Their lyrics were so raunchy that even the A&R people couldn't endure their set, and people literally scattered like terrified birds flying out the door of the Whisky and into the night.

After their set, the lights came up in the bar, and the room was completely empty. Then it started raining. It doesn't rain in Southern California. That fact is well documented. There's even a song about it. But not only did it rain at the worst possible moment, it poured.

Not only had Bardot chased everyone out of the bar, the gully washer ensured that no one from the Roxy would be walking down the street to watch us play.

When our moment came—the moment we'd promised ourselves a year earlier—we took the stage at the Whisky and played our hearts out to an empty bar.

No A&R people, not a soul from the worship event, just us, a bartender, some servers, and the sound engineer.

We didn't let that stop us. We gave our most heartfelt and spirited performance of the summer. The whole time I was in awe that we were there, playing at the Whisky.

We didn't get signed. And, sure, I was disappointed that no one got to hear our impassioned set and that no one stuck around to see our potential or invite us to perform somewhere else. But that's when I knew this was not something I was doing for money or applause. I loved playing with the band, even in an empty room. This was my passion.

But, at the close of the night, one conversation with people in the bar planted a seed that would take years to germinate and grow. Everything I didn't know that night at the Whisky, God did know. I now believe he was there in the middle of that experience, driving the roots of his dream even deeper into my soul—roots that would continue to lead me to be exactly who I am born to be.

If, like me, you've had one of those experiences you just knew would change everything, but then it didn't, you may be wondering as I did at the time, *Why would God let me get so close to what I wanted that I could taste it, without letting me experience the thrill of seeing my hopes come to reality?*

It's easy to misinterpret these moments as God being cruel or withholding, as if he gets some sort of deranged joy out of dangling that dream carrot out in front of us just to trick us in the end. Now I've come to know and trust his heart and can look back on our night at the Whisky with so much more gratitude. The Father gave me this experience, even though I kind of stretched the truth to get us invited there and even though he knew what would happen to Paradigm 5 in a few short months. He knew the plans he had for me, plans not to harm me, but to bring me hope and a future. And in his grace, he allowed me a night at the Whisky as a gift. I can just imagine the joy it brought him to let me fulfill a dream that had been stirring around in me since childhood. I didn't have kids then, but now I think about how I would feel if one of my sons got to make a dream like that happen. I would be weeping tears of joy just watching them have that moment. I imagine him smiling tears of joy as he watched me play my heart out that night.

My friend David Mullins is fond of asking himself the question: "When Jesus isn't the Messiah I want him to be, will I let him be the God I need him to be?" That's what I had to ask myself. When God's plan disappointed me, I had a decision to make. I could reject his plan and go with my own, or trust his love for me enough to let go of my expectations and believe he had a better path for me that would not make my life suck. This is a decision we all have to make. Little did I know how difficult the events of the next couple months would make this decision. Could I chose to let him be God?

*Chapter Eight*

# MURDER IN THE FIRST

After that summer of touring across America, playing gigs every weekend, and writing new songs, we were talking to record companies and radio stations, and it was working. It was growing. We would often borrow a quote from the movie *Almost Famous* and say, "It's all happening!" And it *was* all happening…until it wasn't.

Baltimore, Maryland, is the scene. Paradigm 5 was playing for a buddy's church. Often the band would help lead worship on Sunday morning, after which I would serve as the guest preacher, then the band would stay and do a concert for the youth group that evening. If you grew up in church, you may remember Sunday night youth group. On this particular night in Baltimore, the concert went especially well—it was a great crowd, there was lots of energy, and we sold a ton of band merchandise, which was helpful because the band had become our main source of income.

I still worked part-time at an athletic shoe store during the week, but the band was paying our rent and the rent was coming due. So, off to Maryland we went. Between what we got paid from the church and a great night of merch sales, it was always a relief to know we would be able to pay our rent on time.

So the show was done and we were talking to kids, selling merch, signing autographs, and praying for students who had asked for prayer. In the middle of our post-concert activities, someone came up and told us it looked like someone had ransacked our dressing room. Truthfully, it was a stretch to call it a dressing room. It was really just one of the church's youth ministry rooms, but calling it our dressing room definitely makes the story sound more legit, don't you think?

We went to check on our stuff, and sure enough, our suitcases and bags were all dumped out and scattered around the room, but we were relieved to discover that nothing was missing. Charlie had an expensive watch he left in his bag, but it was still in the bag when he checked. After a few more minutes of investigating, we soon realized the only thing missing was $350 from our cash box. Oddly, our cash box wasn't even in the dressing room. It was in between the front seats of our van. Had someone looked in our dressing room and then somehow, luckily, checked the van to find our cash? It was strange and confusing.

We were bummed; the church was embarrassed and apologetic. But before we left, we circled up and prayed for the person who had stolen the money, acknowledging that maybe they needed that money worse than we did.

Shaken, confused, and upset, we loaded the van and departed. The next day was a scheduled day off, which we had planned to spend in New York City. Not only were we going to drive to the Big Apple, but Charlie had worked at a hotel during that semester and set us up with really nice rooms for a great employee rate. Being able to stay in such nice hotels but actually paying only like $39 a night for our rooms made us feel like rock stars on a college student's budget.

We chose a hotel right next to Times Square so we could spend the entire next day sightseeing and enjoying NYC. We were bummed about the robbery the previous night, but the fun of Times Square was a welcome distraction, and we were grateful for a day off to experience the city together with our dearest friends.

Charlie, however, had a gnawing hunch about the robbery, which he shared with Aaron. Lee was headed home the next morning, so before everyone else woke up, Aaron and Charlie searched again for the money and discovered exactly $350 rolled up and hidden in a sock that belonged to Lee. They had no idea what to do. They didn't say a word.

The next day, Lee left with a friend for home and the rest of us drove from New York back to Indiana. Aaron and Charlie kept the information to themselves throughout the long drive until we finally pulled into our driveway.

That's when Charlie broke the news: "Damon, Daron, there's something we've got to tell you…"

At first I couldn't believe what I was hearing. But there was no other explanation. Lee had stolen the money. My heart sank deeper than I knew it could sink. In that moment, the pain of this betrayal began to settle in and take up residence. Everything that led up to this moment, all our hopes for the future of this band, was in jeopardy. We spent the next couple of days trying to make sense of it all, putting the pieces of the story together, and we were devastated.

We finally told Lee we knew he had stolen the money. He didn't deny it. He went on to explain that he'd gotten into a tough financial situation, and with Christmas approaching, he panicked because he didn't know what else to do. He did apologize. And his reasoning made sense. But that didn't relieve the pain or restore the trust that had been broken.

Walking through this kind of betrayal was uncharted for me. It was tough to make sense of anything, especially since the situation involved a dream that encapsulated so much of my identity. I had never faced anything like this. I suddenly questioned everything. Could I trust anyone? Could I trust myself? Could I trust God?

After Christmas, Lee came back to school and told us he had gone to counseling and talked to his parents about what happened. He assured us we wouldn't have to worry about anything like that happening again. Everything within us wanted to believe him, and we chose to believe him. We loved him. We believed in him and still do to this day.

A few days after the conversation with Lee, I woke to the sound of someone pounding on the front door of our apartment. It was way too early for anybody I considered a friend to be knocking on my door. When I opened it, I was surprised to see two cops in uniform. They informed me there had been a break-in across the street at our friend's house and asked us to come over there immediately. My heart felt like it was going to disintegrate. It had happened again.

I walked up to the house and passed a video player sitting out in the front yard and a lamp sitting on the front steps. I walked in the house to find the TV lying facedown on the carpet and other items disheveled. Police were on the scene, questioning people about their whereabouts during the night.

One of the officers pulled Aaron and me aside and said, "We're going to be honest, guys. We think one of you did this."

Aaron and I looked at each other knowingly, then we simultaneously answered, "Yeah, we do too."

The weeks that followed are honestly a blur. Lee admitted he had taken money from someone who was staying overnight at the house. He unenrolled from school and left town, marking the sudden, painful end of Paradigm 5.

We started going to counseling as a band. Although it was helpful to process the way this betrayal had impacted us individually and as a group, healing took time. In fact, it would take years to fully heal. Not only because Lee had betrayed us, but also because this band of brothers was an important part of our life. We spent every single day together. Our dreams for the future were woven together, and when one of us was lost, we all felt lost.

Years later, Lee came back to Indiana to visit us and apologized for what happened. He had apologized before, but this time we had years of maturity and healing behind us. We forgave him, of course. We loved him and we always will. I can honestly say I don't hold any ill will against Lee now. I did for a long time. He made poor decisions that hurt people and himself. He was going through a tough time. But you know what I realized? I've made bad decisions, too. I've hurt people and myself, too. Like Lee, there have been times when my character was too weak to handle the weight of my dreams. I've betrayed people and have been restored, too.

The irony about this betrayal in the brotherhood is that the very circumstances I blamed for the first-degree murder of my dream also taught me that there is no pain, no betrayal, no poor choice that can't be healed, restored, and redeemed. In fact, Lee, Charlie, and Damon later started a company and worked well together for years.

Healing, restoration, and redemption are always available to us, but God can't do that for us. His heart is always about restoring us, lovingly teaching us, and healing the parts of us that could sabotage our future. But we have to choose it.

Now I understand that I wasn't being penalized or humiliated by God. On a winter day in Indiana, as I walked across the icy campus weeping over the loss of trust and the death of a dream, God's heart broke with me. I believe he wept with Lee, too, and walked with him through the difficult days that followed. The gentle nudges I had followed weren't any less important because of what happened.

I can now say, without reservation, that God's dream for our lives is never about withholding, or punishing, or robbing us of the chance to do what we love. But he uses mistakes, character flaws, broken relationships, and painful circumstances to meet us, heal us, shine his light on our character, and lead us to a place of humility. And we will need all of that to really live a life that brings us joy and him glory. Allowing the light in requires us to unclench our fists and lay our future in the arms of love.

I struggled to do that, though. For a long time, I wasn't ready to let go of control. I thought it was easier to blame others—

or even God—for allowing what I cared about most to unravel right before my eyes. In truth, I chose the most difficult path. Hanging on to that dream was a burden I was never meant to carry. But I refused to lay it down at first.

When asked, "Are you going to leave, too?" I didn't leave. But I also wasn't ready to fully believe that any other plan for my future would be okay.

*Chapter Nine*

# LIFE'S NOT FAIR

You're blessed when you care. At the moment
of being "care-full," you find yourselves cared
for. You're blessed when you get your inside
world—your mind and heart—put right. Then
you can see God in the outside world.

—*Matthew 5:7–8*

f there's one phrase, one sentence, one feeling that I had while
walking through the death of a dream, it was "It's not fair."
The relationships, the band, the traveling, the dream, the conversations we'd been having with recording companies about
record deals—it all came to a grinding halt.

We were graduating from college in three months, and we
had no band, no direction, and no idea what to do next. The
unfairness of it all was overwhelming.

After graduation, I ended up working as a census taker for the summer. Fortunately, I had been warned about this type of disappointment. If I heard it once, I probably heard it ten thousand times from my dad: "Life's not fair."

If you didn't have a dad who told you that, let me be the one to let you know. Life really is not fair. I wish it was. It sure would make things a lot easier.

If the unfairness of life has ever sucker-punched you, I don't have to tell you how hard it is to reckon with. Maybe you feel it in big, obvious ways, like a betrayal by someone you trusted, a major illness or loss, or perhaps a financial disaster. Or maybe you feel it in little ways, like seeing your friend's life on social media and feeling that yours pales in comparison.

Unfairness touches all of us, at some level. Maybe you consistently show up for people who offer zero gratitude or support in return. Maybe you tried to do the right thing at work but got in trouble for it, or you worked hard for a promotion that went to someone else. What about the kid who got a brand-new Jeep Wrangler for their birthday, and you're still driving your dad's old clunker. Or your friend's parents have a seemingly perfect marriage, but your parents got a divorce. Or *that* person can have a few beers at dinner, but if you have a few beers, it becomes a case of beer, and you're gonna wake up in a stranger's car three days later. Sooner or later, the realization forces itself on us that life's not fair—because it just isn't.

So how do we possibly respond? What do we do about it? It's okay to be mad, or sad, or discouraged. We wouldn't be human if we didn't feel whatever we feel when unfair things knock the wind out of us.

We can even stay mad if we want. We can assume that God has left us to fend for ourselves. When life hands us lemons, we can make way too many margaritas and try to numb the pain of how awful we feel. Or we can attempt to take control of everything and make things work out for ourselves, even if it means lying, fighting, stealing, cheating, or working ourselves to death. I've tried these options. These options are survival mode options that will eventually leave us tired, isolated, and maybe even in rehab. These options are fueled by the assumption that we have to figure this out on our own.

Accepting the reality that life is not fair is far more bearable when we know we are *not* alone in it. Ever. We can choose to trust that God is *with* us and *for* us and lean into the reality that he is—even right this minute—working on our behalf in ways that we can't see yet. When we learn that we can fully lean into God's character, we gain a renewed energy to live and live freely without scorekeeping, withholding, or trying to take control.

The choice is ours. We can choose the role of the victim, which leads us to become people we don't even like. Or we can step into the role of the resilient, beloved leading character in the story of our life. We can ask for the strength and wisdom God has promised to everyone who asks for it, and we can accept hope that is ours for the asking.

God promises that he is always for us and always near us, and when we live life on his terms, we come to understand that every unfair thing life serves up has within it the potential to deepen our resolve to live an epic, holy, loving, gracious, compassionate story. Those qualities don't just happen. We nurture them every time we take God at his word and step further into trust that his love is stronger than the unfairness of life.

God knows more about feeling betrayed than we could ever fathom. In those moments when life is unkind, or even downright cruel, we have a capacity to connect with his unconditional love at depths we never could if life's fairness scorecard was always leaning in our favor.

Let's catch up with Joseph to see how his dream is going, because if anybody's journey proves that life's not fair, it's Joseph's. Remember, when we left off with Joseph his dream had died when his brothers betrayed him and left him in a pit to die. But guess what: God was still with Joseph.

When we find ourselves in a pit, we have to remember what God is constantly communicating to us. This truth is made very clear in James 1:2–4: "Consider it a sheer gift, friends, when tests and challenges come at you from all sides. You know that under pressure, your faith-life is forced into the open and shows its true colors. So don't try to get out of anything prematurely. Let it do its work so you become mature and well-developed, not deficient in any way."

Unfair or unfavorable circumstances are always an invitation to character development. We see this through Joseph's story, and I can confirm this to be true in my own story as well. The death of "how things were supposed to go" according to our plans eventually becomes an invitation to endurance, to tapping into power and vision far beyond our own.

The process of becoming who you were born to be means living with the reality that Jesus is way more invested in who you are becoming than he is in making you feel warm and fuzzy.

His plan always includes developing your character so you can be strong enough to carry the weight of your calling. Building strength of character is not easy work. But it's the only way to align ourselves with his ultimate purposes for our lives.

In Joseph's story, he was literally at the bottom of a pit, thanks to his jealous brothers. They left him there because they felt they had been treated unfairly. They chose option one. They took matters into their own hands because they felt it was the only way to even the score between them and Joseph. The way their father treated them *was* unfair.

Genesis 36 tells us when the Midianite traders arrived in Egypt, they sold Joseph to Potiphar, who was an officer of Pharaoh, the king of Egypt. What nobody except God knew in this situation was that a famine was coming. This famine would be so severe that it threatened to wipe out all of God's people. The good news in this story and in yours is that God had and has promised to provide for and protect his covenant people. God's plan was to place someone in authority to lead and guide Egypt and to provide the food, protection, and provision to save not only God's people but all of the Egyptian people. So in the midst of his brothers' betrayal, Joseph was being prepared by God for great power and authority.

Joseph goes from being thrown into a pit to being given a job in an Egyptian palace—pretty good upgrade from the pit to the palace. God saw beyond that pit and used it to put Joseph exactly where he needed him to be.

Genesis 39:2 (NLT) says, "The Lord was with Joseph." Don't miss that. This is no small declaration. The God who created and sustains the entire universe was personally invested in Joseph's journey. He was with him. Was this fair? No, he wasn't with his family. He wasn't in his land. He had been betrayed by his brothers. He would have every reason to believe his life was over, but the Lord was with Joseph.

Then the verse continues: "so he succeeded in everything he did." As he served the role he was given, he did it all, and his master, Potiphar, noticed this. He could see that the Lord's favor was with Joseph. Since everything he was given to do turned out successfully, Potiphar made Joseph his personal attendant and put him in charge of his entire household and everything he owned. And the day Joseph was put in charge of his master's household and property, the Lord began to bless Potiphar's household for Joseph's sake. All his household affairs ran smoothly, and he knew he could trust Joseph. This is a beautiful moment.

At this point, I'm sure there were days when Joseph thought, "Wow, God is with me. This has all worked out!" And then he lived happily ever after. But that isn't at all the end of the story. In fact, life got even more unfair for Joseph.

Scripture tells us that Joseph was a good-looking dude. Unfortunately, Potiphar's wife noticed this and tried to seduce him into bed with her. Joseph's character was strong and he resisted, but in a stroke of unbelievable unfairness, Potiphar's wife accused him of sexual assault when he rejected her advances. When Potiphar heard about her accusations, he was furious. He had Joseph thrown into prison with the king's other prisoners and remained there for years. Talk about unfair!

Here's another opportunity for Joseph to play the victim. He could have thrown his hands into the air and said, "See?! God can't be trusted! He doesn't come through. I'm on my own. I've got to take care of myself because obviously no one else will!"

Blaming God or other people wreaks havoc on our hearts, our souls, and our emotions. We inevitably find ourselves over-whelmed and anxious, constantly overthinking, sleep-deprived, in need of peace and rest, and susceptible to depression. When we get into that kind of tailspin, we tend to get on a mental tread-mill that convinces us that we have to figure out the way forward all by ourselves. But that's a lie that runs completely counter to the truth of who God says he is.

Joseph has gone from the pit to the palace to the prison, but the Lord never left Joseph. Even in prison, he showed his faithful love and made Joseph a favorite with the prison warden. And, in another strange plot twist, Pharaoh's baker and cupbearer end up in prison with him. The warden put them with Joseph and gave him the responsibility of looking after them. While there, the baker and cupbearer both had bizarre dreams, and Joseph's interpretation of their dreams proved correct: The cupbearer would return to his position in Pharoah's court, and the baker would be killed. In return for his interpretation of their dreams, he asked the cupbearer to remember him when he returned to Pharaoh. But when the cupbearer was released from prison, the cupbearer forgot all about him.

At any point in his story, I wouldn't be surprised to read that Joseph tapped out. If you have ever watched a UFC fight, the phrase *tapping out* is a familiar one. When a competitor puts an opponent into a submission hold, he basically tries to choke the life out of the opponent, break his arm, or something else really painful. When the opponent has taken all he can stand

and reaches his quitting point, he signifies his surrender by tapping the ground or the opponent. The moment he taps out, the struggle, the suffocation, the fight ends. But so does the chance at victory. Tapping out means you recognize that you've lost the fight.

There's nothing quite like watching a fight where someone finds themself in the seemingly impossible rear naked choke gasping for air, then they manage to hang on until the end of the round. After every attempt to take he or she down, they keep coming back for another round, and another. Then, when they are tired of losing, you see something shift. They start to rally and then make a miraculous comeback! I think the reason I love watching those fights is because they remind me of the numerous times when my life felt like a UFC fight. I could have easily tapped out numerous times because I was so tired of fighting. Even when it felt like a losing battle, I would have moments that reminded me to not leave—to just stay in there fighting.

I'm sure Joseph felt like tapping out plenty of times. And any human with a beating heart would have understood. At any point in our lives, we have the freedom to walk away from God. He doesn't force us to follow, because love isn't love if we don't have the ability to choose to stay in the ring. That fact kind of scares me, honestly, because I know very well what happens if I tap out. It means I forfeit the opportunity to see what's possible when I've done all I know to do then something—or Someone— else takes over and turns everything around. There is nowhere we can go to escape his presence. We're told in Psalm 139:7 that we never escape from his Spirit. But tapping out means we miss out on the chance to rely on his strength when our own is gone.

But staying in the ring is the only way to find out how his power can carry us to the finish.

Joseph didn't play the victim. He clearly knew God was with him and that his story was not over. He served people in the palace, and then he served people in prison. He couldn't have done that if he was playing the role of a victim. He knew he wasn't alone, even when circumstances seemed all wrong.

Imagine what Jacob, Joseph's father, must have been experiencing for all those years. Can you imagine what he must have been thinking as he saw what was happening in his family? His sons betrayed him, lied to him, and sold his favorite son into slavery, and the whole time Joseph was in Egypt, Jacob thought he was dead. He, too, would eventually see God's faithfulness and his redemption because his son didn't tap out.

I also imagine how God must have felt as his son hung in the balance between life and death. The injustice of it all must have broken the Father's heart. Talk about unfair. No one understands the death of our dreams more than God. I believe his heart breaks every time ours do. Even though he knows the future, and even though he is the very definition of love, he surely grieves the pain of injustice.

Jesus had the opportunity to tap out if he wanted. He could have done a miracle for himself at any moment to avoid the pain he experienced. But he didn't. The dream was far bigger than his thirty-three year journey on this planet with us.

This kind of attitude and trust are possible when you invite his presence into your inside world—deep in your mind and heart. When you see your broken dreams from his divine perspective, you realize God didn't bring unfairness into your life.

He felt the pain of injustice more deeply than we'll ever know. Even still, every unfair thing brings an opportunity for that internal shift from victim to victor.

Think of everything good or bad that has happened in your life. If you want, you can explain it all away as series of coincidences. But that way of thinking would mean you're alone, that God is distant or nonexistent, and that your whole life has been left to fate or chance. But when you realize that your circumstances never once caused him to leave, you can't help but realize that you are never actually alone. If you aren't alone now, you never have been. The wonderful Counselor has been here the whole time. That's a big deal. That is what makes him the Hope of the Ages.

Generations ago, nomadic people gained security and provision by striking covenants with other tribes and groups of people. We see this in the Old Testament story of Abraham and Melchizedek, and then ultimately with Abraham and Yahweh. The basic terms of their covenants were that the more powerful person entering the covenant promised on their life to protect and provide for the weaker, less powerful person in the covenant. Within the covenant ceremony, an animal was sacrificed and cut in half. Gross, I know. But that's how they rolled back then. And, odd as it sounds, the participants in the covenant would walk between the two halves, pledging to the covenant to protect and provide for one another. Then they shared a meal of bread and wine.

The covenant signified a merging of strength and weakness, needs and provision. It wasn't made because of fairness, but out of care and love to provide safety and peace between both parties. They took these covenants seriously, and they signified a new beginning—together.

Culturally, most of us are more familiar with a covenant in the context of marriage. It's a commitment intended for life where each person's strengths and weaknesses come together to create something new: a place where safety and peace are nurtured so neither person has to be alienated or alone for the rest of their lives. The marriage covenant is a reflection of the New Covenant that Christ came to fulfill. In the Old Testament covenant, God promised to protect and provide for the people of Israel. But in the New Covenant that Christ made possible, we can experience the protection and provision of his presence not only for the rest of our lives, but for eternity. It isn't based on anything we have earned, and it signifies a new beginning where we can begin the rest of our life knowing he is always there and we never have to try to even the score. We are given the chance to trust him enough to leave the outcomes to him. This is far less terrifying if we know how much he loves us and how trustworthy he is.

If there is one thing we need to believe when we are navigating the unfairness of life, it is that our struggles are not in vain. We need to know there are no coincidences. We need to be able to believe the covenant is there for our benefit. When we experience painful circumstances, we can look to Joseph's story and Jesus's story and take heart.

When things do not get better overnight, knowing that God is *with* us and *for* us gives us the ability to invite him into our inner world. This is how we can find joy and purpose that goes beyond our external circumstances. This is where we discover how his strength is demonstrated in our weakness. When our faith is tested, as Joseph's was, we can either tap out and miss the entire purpose he is trying to accomplish, or we can release the need for control and let his power sustain us so we can endure whatever comes knowing we are part of a far bigger plan than we might realize.

Listen, my friend, life will never be fair. But your greatest Advocate is generous and gracious. He has literally felt your pain. And because of that pain, he made a covenant for all eternity to never leave you high and dry. His covenant love for you will take you to places you never thought possible.

You may be confused about what to do next, so ask him for wisdom. James 1:5–6 (NIV) says, "If any of you lacks wisdom, you should ask God, who gives generously to all without finding fault, and it will be given to you."

You may be mad, so ask him to overwhelm you with generous grace. Whether or not it makes sense, just know that he is developing in you exactly what you'll need to fulfill your life's purposes.

Whatever you do, stay in the ring. Don't tap out.

*Chapter Ten*

# LET IT DIE

I attended an Audio Adrenaline concert during their Festival con Dios tour. I think it was in 2001 or 2002—just a year plus removed from the death of my dream. The pain and grief were still pretty fresh. However, attending live concerts is always my happy place, so I decided to attend. I didn't speak Spanish but concluded that the translation of Festival con Dios must mean "a parking lot by the church." It was bittersweet to be there because, at one time, our band had been considered for an opening slot on that tour.

While the crowd enjoyed the music, I was engaged in a bitter argument with God. I was asking all the usual questions again: Why this? Why not? Why me? All of my questions were predicated on the false belief that God didn't have my best interests at heart. I guess that's always the lie. Sure, God did amazing things in the past, but for some reason it's hard to believe he could still do all that and more in the future.

During my stand-off with God in that parking lot, Audio Adrenaline started to play a song that might as well have featured the voice of God on lead vocals. Because, as I listened, I knew I was hearing his usual question for me, this time with different words. It was in that parking lot in the year 2002 that I once again faced the question "Do you want to leave too?"

The gentle nudge of the Father encouraged me to let my dream go, let it die, and embrace something better. God couldn't do something better until I let go. It was time to stop and recognize that he was doing a new thing in what felt like the middle of the desert. That night, I laid down the dream and experienced the overwhelming presence of God's Spirit. For the first time in forever, I felt peace.

The tough thing about making our lives a "living sacrifice" like Paul writes about in Romans 12 is that living sacrifices can crawl off the altar. So yeah, that night I laid down my life and my dream on the altar of God. It wouldn't be too long after that I picked it back up and crawled away. I crawled away many, many times. The hardest thing about sacrificing and submitting my life to a power greater than myself is that I would always be human. I would have to relearn trust over and over again.

I wish I could go back and change that, but that's the point. Unfortunately, or perhaps very fortunately, we can't go backward. We can only move forward. We can choose either redemption or regret. In time I learned to choose redemption.

When a dream that defined you, identified you, drove you, had become you is finally pronounced dead…then what? This is a dilemma millions of people find themselves facing. We have to muster up enough courage to relearn how to live.

In the face of relearning how to live, it's tempting to retreat—to shrink back from feeling vulnerable. When we have been wounded, when our confidence has been shaken, and all that remains is the lifeless skeleton of a dream that once filled every day with meaning and purpose, do you know what we do next? We have a funeral. We gather together with the ones we love, empty a box of Kleenex, and let it out. We cry it out, hug it out, tell stories, and celebrate the good, and then we say goodbye. We celebrate, mourn, and then let…it…die.

Did you ever meet somebody who is obviously living in the past? It's awkward. And usually easy to pick out. Maybe it's their clothes, makeup, or hairstyle—can you say mullet? But most often the issue runs much deeper than someone's outer appearance. Often the outer appearance points to a person's struggle to leave an era of their life in the past. Maybe they don't recognize themself without those glimpses of the person they wanted to be, or used to be.

Anyway, that was pretty much me. I kept trying to pull off that rock star vibe, complete with the chip on my shoulder that had been with me for so many years.

When we experience loss, pain, or trauma that results in the death of a dream, it's easy to get stuck, to live in it, and even to become identified with it. In order to be the person we were born to be, it's important to separate the things that happen to us from our being. I had to learn that I am not my circumstances.

We are not our pain, loss, or former dreams. For me, learning to rediscover myself required a different understanding of myself and God. Just as I cannot go back in time, God isn't stuck in the past where things went wrong. Sure, we can see his faithfulness by looking back, but his presence is experienced right here and now. And when we learn to just be and allow his presence to just be with us in this moment, we can better understand his passion for creating a future that is built moment by moment.

When the final semester of my college career came to a close, my dream was in the proverbial ICU, hooked up to life support. Unfortunately, I kept it there for the next decade. The humane thing to do would have been to just let it die quietly. But that isn't what I did. I tried more than once to revive it. We connected with someone who had a production deal with a record company in Nashville. The four remaining band members argued for a month over what we should do, and we were split, two and two. Half of us wanted to go to Nashville, and half of us wanted to stay in Indiana. Without Lee, there was no swing vote. So we came to a stalemate. One of us moved to Nashville. Three of us stayed in Indiana. But the recording opportunity came and went.

During that time, we also made our first attempt at restoring our relationship with Lee and decided to get the band back together to open for the band Delirious? in Fort Wayne, Indiana. The show was in an outdoor amphitheater. We had never played a venue that large, and we had never opened for a band that well known. It was an amazing, emotional night. It was also the largest gig of our short career. I should have been willing to finish on a high note and let go of my version of what the dream needed to look like. But, no, I was stubborn. I wanted what I wanted too badly. I wanted to tell God what I was willing to do for him rather than actually be open to what he could do in me and through me.

There is a movie made back in 1989 called *Weekend at Bernie's* where two young dudes are houseguests of a guy named Bernie. Somehow Bernie dies, and they spend the whole weekend lugging Bernie around, trying to convince people he's still alive. The slapstick humor with the dead body makes for a stupid movie with a lot of junior high humor, but I can't help but see how Bernie signified my dream for so long. I kept trying to prop it up and make it seem great, but nothing could change the reality that it was dead. I'm sure it probably seemed laughable from others' perspectives, but I can now look back at that season of my life and see how much it resembled a dumb movie plot.

It's scary to let something we love die. Jesus had some dear friends, Mary, Martha, and their brother, Lazarus, who experienced a major death of a dream. There are several stories about Jesus's friendship with Martha and Mary. In fact, Mary was the same woman who anointed Jesus's feet with perfume and dried them off with her hair, which was a rare and intimate ritual reflecting her deep affection for Jesus. In John 11, we're told that they lived in the village of Bethany, and they sent someone from the village to go find Jesus because Lazarus was sick and they were afraid he was going to die.

"The one you love is very sick. Please come." The messenger pleaded with Jesus.

Like many of our stories, this one gets worse, or at least odd, before it gets better. "Jesus loved Martha and her sister and Lazarus, but oddly, when he heard that Lazarus was sick, he stayed on where he was for two more days" (John 11:6). "But oddly"? Jesus remained where he was for two more days. His friend is on his deathbed, and he stays away for two more days?

Yeah, I would say that's odd. It just doesn't make sense. I'm guessing you've had a "but oddly" moment with Jesus? You have read about his love. You have experienced his love, much like Mary, Martha, and Lazarus, and still Jesus isn't showing up when and how you would choose. Oddly enough, life still isn't fair. Oddly enough, the dream is still dead. It is in these "oddly enough" moments that our faith and trust in Jesus are tested.

When he finally shows up, Mary and Martha are beside themselves and tell Jesus he is too late. They had to be thinking the same thing all of us wonder at some point: If Jesus loves us so much, why would he let this happen? Jesus loved his friend. And his friend died. It would be hard not to be mad at him, knowing he could have prevented this. Isn't the love of God supposed to keep anything bad from ever happening to me? Doesn't God's love guarantee a life without pain and disappointment? No, it doesn't. In fact, Jesus even told us in this life we would have struggles of many kinds. But he also encouraged us by saying, "But take heart! I have overcome the world" (John 16:33 NIV).

When he finally comes to Mary and Martha, they are grieving. They tell Jesus, "If you had only been here, our brother wouldn't have died!" Here is the really tough part about moments like this in our lives: Mary and Martha are probably right. If Jesus had come early, he could have healed Lazarus before he died. But oddly enough, he didn't. It seems that Jesus knew, as he always knows, how to bring about the greatest good. His ways are always above our ways. His plans are always good. Jesus always has your best interest at heart, even in the odd and painful moments of life.

If you know the story, you know that one of the most powerful moments happens next. As Jesus sees their pain and feels the
sadness of the loss, Jesus weeps. Jesus doesn't condemn them
for their sorrow. He doesn't stop their grief and say, "Stop feeling this pain now, because I'm about to do something good."
Even with the knowledge of the miracle he is about to do, Jesus
weeps with those he loves when their hearts are overwhelmed
with sorrow. You might need to pause and read that again. In
your heartbreak, sorrow, and confusion about the death of your
dream, Jesus offers compassion, empathy, and presence. He
weeps with you.

That is good news. Here's better news. Jesus doesn't just
have a heart that weeps with us. Jesus also has the power to heal
and resurrect our hearts. Jesus weeps with Mary and Martha and
then raises their brother from the dead! Imagine their elation
when Jesus called out to Lazarus, and next thing you know he
was walking out of his own tomb! More than two thousand years
later, we are still talking about how Jesus let him die and how
it seemed like all hope was lost. But a better story was about to
happen. Death never is actually the end of the story with Jesus.

Even when we don't get it, if we are willing to trust Jesus
with our dreams, we will eventually experience the joy of resurrection. Dreams have a life cycle. They have a birth, a life, and a
death. But here's the best part: Dreams also have a resurrection.
They may take on a different appearance. Not even Jesus's closest friends recognized him after his resurrection.

When you let your dream die and leave it in Jesus's hands,
you may not recognize it at first when it rises from the mist. But
the real miracles only happen when you stop trying to figure

it all out and let it go. That is when God can take the abilities, talents, and determination that has been knit into your DNA and accomplish things through you that you never thought possible.

He cares immeasurably more about who you are becoming than he does about what you are accomplishing. God's greatest dream for your life is to see you become all that you've been created to be. That dream has everything to do with your character and very little to do with your career.

So if you're staring at the corpse of a dream, take it from me: Don't prolong its agony. It's time for a funeral. Mourn the loss, refocus your life on your true identity, and allow yourself to prepare for a resurrection when you will finally realize the dream was always about your transformation. Save yourself more heartache and let that dream die, so you can experience the resurrection of the purpose you were created to fulfill.

*Chapter Eleven*

# THE CRUX

For the next couple of years I tried to figure out what life without the dream was going to look like. As I ever so slowly let go of the dream I once had, I also felt it being pried from my hands in some ways. These guys I planned to conquer the world with were finding jobs in other parts of the country, and we were all trying to make sense of how to apply our gifts and abilities to other kinds of settings. I would learn that drumming was not the dream; it was the means through which I would unearth my deeper passion for helping people discover life with Jesus. I was still passionate about reaching people in ways that felt unique and creative. I would always love music. But I also learned that I had other gifts, too, and I'd been too busy making music to see them before. Through gifts of leadership and speaking, God began inviting me into new dreams. The more I let go of the dream I started with, the more I realized that dream was way too small.

In the fall of 2001 I started a young adult ministry and had a vision to grow it into a new church that would appeal to young adults who didn't like church. I still longed to invite people to have spiritual conversations, but it wouldn't be at concerts at rock clubs. I wanted to develop a creative place that engaged people spiritually and drew them with the love and truth of Jesus.

I dreamed big, believing this fresh approach to church could easily become a movement. I wanted to see us reach our community, then plant campuses in all four corners of Indianapolis. I dreamed of it becoming a church that sent people on missions all over the world for years to come. It was an audacious dream. But I didn't have much to start it with.

At the time I was doing an internship at a church making $8,000 a year. Yes, a total $8,000 for an entire year. I had also fallen in love with a beautiful Southern spitfire named Julie. I knew I wanted to marry her. So to make this dream happen and to start my life with Julie, I was going to need a financial miracle.

Every Tuesday, I met with a spiritual mentor, Dr. Foley, for breakfast. One Tuesday, over eggs and bacon, we were talking about the church idea, and I told him I was passionate about starting the church but couldn't survive on what I'd been making during the internship. He was excited about the vision and asked me how much money I would need to begin.

When I told him, Dr. Foley responded, "If I start writing the checks next month, will you start this church?"

Ten months after that conversation we pioneered a church called The Crux. On September 16, 2001, we held our first service. It was the first Sunday after the terrorist attacks on the

World Trade Center in New York City on September 11, 2001—a heavy but memorable week to launch a new church.

The Crux was named after the Latin word for cross. A crux is a point of resolution. That was my heart. I wanted to bring people to the cross of Jesus so they could find resolution and meaning in their lives. I hoped they would find clarity on God's unconditional love for them and on who he had created them to be.

The Crux doubled in size every year for the first four years. Before you get too excited about that level of growth, keep in mind that we started with only thirty-nine people on our first Sunday. But nonetheless, it was growing, and I loved what we were building. I had found a new passion and a dream that was less about me and what I wanted to do and more about helping others and fulfilling God's dream for the world.

Over the next six years, The Crux gradually became my everything. I still hadn't learned how to keep my dreams from determining my identity. Figuring that one out is a lifelong journey, I now know.

What I also didn't know about myself yet is that I am an Enneagram 7/ENFP/Pioneer/Apostle according to some assessments that helped me understand more about how I'm wired. All those qualities basically mean that I like starting things, I like freedom, and I like having choices and options. I don't like to feel trapped, and I have a hard time being told no. My life motto is "more is better," and one teeny-tiny detail that eventually became obvious is that I'm a better speaker than I am a pastor.

After six years of leading The Crux, my job had become indistinguishable from my identity, and I was having what I call a missional freak-out. It all started with a Cubs game and a beer.

My neighbor Chad and I both loved the Cubs. And he loved beer. I didn't drink any alcohol at that point because my church denomination—which was the same affiliation as my college, all my churches growing up, and this new church I was planting—prohibited alcohol consumption. Chad worked the early shift at a local sporting goods store as a manager, and he would get home from work midafternoon, usually watch a Cubs game in his garage, and drink some beer.

On this particular afternoon, Chad invited me over to watch the game and have a beer with him. I turned down the beer but was excited to just hang out with Chad and watch the game. For some reason, our conversations felt forced. It was odd. I felt out of place. I am not typically a shy, awkward person, but I came up with a reason to leave early because I felt like something was wrong.

Julie and I had been married for a few years at this point, and she was (and still is) always someone who tells me the truth. So when I got home, I explained to her how odd and uncomfortable I felt hanging out with Chad.

Julie looked at me and, in her usual direct and honest way, said, "That's because you're not a real person anymore." She went on to explain that unless I was at church or talking to church people, I didn't know how to act like a normal human being. I had become like a Pastor Daron cartoon character.

As hard as it was to hear what she was saying, I knew she was right. I had allowed my role as Pastor Daron to overshadow everything else. Without that role, I didn't know who I was or what to talk about other than myself and my church. But I no longer enjoyed it.

I still genuinely wanted to communicate the love of Jesus in everyday spaces and places where people were just living life. I was wired with all the gifts to speak and build bridges with people who were spiritually searching, but when I got honest, I realized I didn't have meaningful relationships with anybody who didn't believe as I did. I was missing the entire point of what I was trying to build. So yes, I freaked out.

Also during my freak-out, the other two pastors on staff with me at The Crux resigned—on the same day. They didn't stage a walkout or anything. The worship pastor's new wife was from Atlanta, and they wanted to move back to the area. So when a position opened up at her home church, he took it. He was planning on resigning at the end of a day we spent traveling to and from a one-day conference in Ohio. But that morning, before we left, my executive pastor sent us an email letting us know he would be leaving to go start a church. He had been hoping to start a church for a while. So throughout the trip that day, we talked about the executive pastor leaving. Then, when we got back to the church that evening he said, "Hey, can we talk for a minute?"

I was losing my staff. And I was losing myself. Oh, and Julie and I had just had our second baby and my mom had just been diagnosed with breast cancer. Looking back I guess this time of life was a little more intense than I realize. I knew I was more than just Pastor Daron, but I couldn't figure out how to just be me anymore. Julie had called it. But I didn't know where to find me again.

So I took a trip to Bosnia. I thought if I went to a country where no one knew who I was or how I was perceived at home, maybe I would find something genuine inside myself that I'd forgotten was there. During my days in Bosnia I helped a team refurbish classrooms that had been damaged in the Bosnian war. Then, at night, our team would visit local coffee shops and learn more about the local culture.

I don't believe for one minute that God plays hide and seek. He has promised that he will never leave us. His presence is always available. He wants to be found. We just have to look for him. I finally did that on a balcony overlooking an abandoned lot at my hotel in Bosnia.

That afternoon, after we finished all our work for the day, I went back to my hotel room to relax. I sat out on the balcony enjoying a cool afternoon breeze, looked around me, and took in my surroundings. Just me, myself, and I...and a burned-out car on blocks, a random cow, and a tree. I wouldn't necessarily describe it as a "room with a view." But as I sat there thinking, reflecting, and praying, I recalled the verse I had dubbed my "life verse" ever since that youth camp where Jimmy Johnson spoke. As I sat alone that day in Bosnia, a gentle nudge seemed to be asking, "What's your life verse again?"

"I know what my life verse is, thank you," I replied.

Kindly and gently, the nudge came again: "Why don't you go get your Bible and read it again?"

The only Bible I had brought to Bosnia was The Message version. And that afternoon, as I read the words of Matthew 11:28–30, I felt as if God himself was sitting next to me on that balcony, lingering in that breeze and speaking directly into my soul.

Are you tired? Worn out? Burned out on religion? Come to me. Get away with me and you'll recover your life. I'll show you how to take

a real rest. Walk with me and work with me—
watch how I do it. Learn the unforced rhythms
of grace. I won't lay anything heavy or ill-fitting
on you. Keep company with me and you'll learn
to live freely and lightly.

As I read these words, I was overwhelmed by the compassion and personal nature of God. I was, indeed, so tired and so worn out. I was definitely burned out on religion and had worked so hard—too hard—to prove myself to God—or rather, to myself. I recalled the night years earlier when I decided to get my yoke on and pursue ministry, I thought about all that had happened since, and I wept. I had lost the point of it all. I had completely missed the joy of simply walking in alignment with Jesus. I'd been too focused on working, accomplishing, proving, and striving. I kept reading Jesus's words and saw something I had missed before: his invitation.

"Come to me. Get away with me and you'll recover your life."

This invitation was what I had come to Bosnia looking for. I had been "working for" Jesus for most of my life. I thought that was what he wanted most. But as I kept reading I realized "walking with" Jesus was the point. The "working with" was secondary.

I kept reading and crying.

"Learn the unforced rhythms of grace." These words felt like a fresh, cold drink of water for my dehydrated soul. I wasn't very familiar with grace. I guess I'd been too focused on forcing rhythms of my own—both literally and figuratively. I didn't yet know how to live in the unforced rhythms of grace. But that afternoon on a balcony in Bosnia, I began to rediscover who God is and, in doing so, rediscovered those lost parts of myself.

Later that week in Bosnia, the team met at our missionary host's home church, and I shared the vulnerable moments I had experienced on the balcony a few days earlier. The others prayed for me to have courage to move from my false sense of self and receive the yoke that could bring me relief on many levels. That experience was a turning point unlike anything I'd ever experienced before.

On our last night in Bosnia, after the team had finished our work, we went out to one of the area's amazing coffee shops. In Bosnia, coffee shops turn into bars after five o'clock. We hung out for hours taking in the culture and enjoying conversations. At midnight the shop closed and the missionaries asked if we were done for the night or if we wanted to take in some more culture.

If you know me at all by now, you know I'm not missing an afterparty for anything. As I already said, my personality can pretty much be summarized by the phrase *more is always better*. I was all in for whatever was next.

Our group walked out of the bar and immediately found ourselves in the middle of what seemed like an organized parade. Mingling into a crowd of partiers, we made our way down the city's cobblestone streets. Up ahead were dance clubs, and people began to pour into the clubs.

We poked our heads into the door of the first club we came to and saw what seemed to be a foam party going on. Music was pumping, and foam was everywhere. As we stood at the entrance, trying to figure out what we were seeing, a horrible smell smacked us in the face, which I can only compare to the odor a wet pack of wolves might generate if they had a dance party. With a unanimous no we went back out onto the street and followed the crowd to another club.

The next place we came to was less foamy but smoky. And when I say "smoky" I don't mean "a few people smoking cigarettes" smoky. I mean "billowing out the front door" smoky. I'm not sure if it's still a thing now, but in 2007, Bosnian young adults loved their cigarettes.

We lasted for a couple of songs, until my contacts felt like they had melted onto my eyeballs. So we headed outside and breathed in some fresh air on the curb near the front door of the club. That's when it hit me. I was halfway around the world in the small town of Livno, Bosnia, and the same thing that was happening there was happening in cities and towns across the planet. Young adults who had no interest in attending church were filling up bars and dance clubs.

I'd worn myself out trying to get young adults who didn't know Jesus into to The Crux, and they were not coming. But what if we could find a way to meet them where they were already gathering?

I mentioned this to one of the missionaries and said, "If we could find a way to own the room in there, we might be able to make a difference." Then, I was struck with the realization that I already knew how to own the room. We learned that lesson through all the bars gigs in the Paradigm 5 days. I came home with a new vision and dream to take Jesus to people where they were already gathering, rather than trying to attract them to church. I left Bosnia wearing a new yoke from Jesus and feeling that my dream had been resurrected.

My old bandmate, Charlie, had been working as a worship pastor in California.

Long story short, he agreed to move his family to Indiana so he could serve as the new worship pastor at The Crux.

So, you'll never believe what I did next. Actually, yes you will believe it. I found a way to get Paradigm 5 back together, minus Lee. We convinced a friend of ours that he could sing and made him our lead singer, and we started playing in bars with a couple-thousand-watt sound system. Note: If you have to convince someone he can sing and you amplify that voice with a couple thousand watts, the result may not be optimal. We figured if anyone in the place didn't like church or thought God was unapproachable, we could give them a different taste of what faith can look like. And we did that with all our energy.

As I met people in bars, with the all the right intentions of meeting them where they were, I started drinking with them. I had consumed almost zero alcohol in my life up to that point, but I didn't want to come across as self-righteous or give the impression that I was a typical pastor. I was in a band and I drank. Surely that would make me more relatable.

This approach to connecting with people worked immediately. When I sat down with people over a drink, conversations opened up about how they were really doing. Words flowed easily, walls came down, and it was easy to have spiritual conversations without defensiveness or fear.

There was just one problem. No one in my denomination's leadership could know I was drinking. So I hid the drinking from anyone who might have a problem with it or report it to my authorities, because I didn't want to lose my ministry credentials.

My intention was to remove the obstacles between others, myself, and God. Although I was trying to reach people for all the right reasons, I was deceptive in the way I did it. Once again, I was doing the dream my way. I didn't want to be told what to do or how to do it.

Apparently a two-thousand-watt sound system in a bar is not an effective way to fly under the radar, because the leadership committee of the denomination found out. They called a meeting where I had to account for my actions and reprimanded me. I apologized, and in order to be allowed to continue as a pastor at The Crux, I had to officially agree to their no-drinking policy for as long as I was part of the denomination.

At this point, my wife and I had already made the decision that we would be leaving The Crux. We no longer wanted to remain in that denomination. I didn't stop pastoring at The Crux because of alcohol. I left because I didn't fit into that denomination anymore for all kinds of reasons. I was being drawn to new frontiers and was looking for a new place to live out my calling. So I resigned from The Crux.

Two weeks before our final Sunday at The Crux, Julie and I attended a Brad Paisley concert with our best friends, Brent and Lesleigh. Knowing I had already resigned and was leaving the denomination in two weeks, I celebrated with a beer at the concert. Two beers, actually.

On the Monday morning following the concert, I received a phone call from the Indiana district superintendent of my denomination. He informed me that a pastor's wife who knew us had attended the same concert that weekend and saw me drinking beer. She informed the leadership, and the district superintendent solemnly proceeded to remind me that I had been given a warning the first time, but this time would require disciplinary action. A few hours later, another phone conversation delivered the verdict that I would not be allowed to speak or preach again at The Crux, or any other church in our denominational network.

The next week would be my last Sunday at The Crux, and I would have the opportunity to say goodbye. But that was all I could say. I stood briefly to deliver my final words and walked away from another dream, utterly discouraged. My original dream died because of circumstances beyond my control. But the responsibility for this one coming to an end was on me.

A few weeks later, I received a letter in the mail to officially notify me that my ministerial credentials had been revoked by the denomination. The letter stated that I had been "disposed of for ministry." That is a direct quote. Having my ministry credentials revoked was hard, even without the sentence reiterating that I had been "disposed of." But the feeling of being discarded…disposed of…removed felt like salt being poured into an open wound.

I knew the letter wasn't from God. It was from a group of imperfect people just like me. I also knew deep down that God's purposes and gifts are irrevocable. But they were no longer applicable within the only denomination I had known since birth. I grieved that reality.

Mingled with the grief and loss were some important lessons for me. The finality of that letter closed the door on a huge part of my life and some close relationships, yet the next door hadn't fully opened yet. That in-between space was lonely and disheartening, yet I knew I had broken a promise and a policy. I knew their expectations. I couldn't deny that.

"God gives grace to the willing humble," according to James 4:6, but I had to choose humility. I was learning the hard way what I told you a few chapters ago, that if I did not choose humility, life would continue to humiliate me. Or, more accurately, I would continue to humiliate myself. I would learn that choosing humility is hard, but letting life humiliate you is much harder.

The Crux closed its doors forever less than eighteen months after we left. There was a whole lot of fallout. I hoped the work we accomplished made a fraction of the impact I had envisioned, but from where I was sitting, I saw mostly failure. That final attempt to resurrect the college kid's version of my dream had, once again, ended tragically.

In time, at a very personal level, The Crux eventually lived up to its name and resulted in resolution of things that needed to be worked out in my character. I believe others who were involved might be able to say the same thing now. But it was devastating at the time.

If I could go back and change any of it, I can honestly say I wouldn't change the outcomes. I wish I could change how I handled things. But I am grateful for the opportunity to learn from my failures, regardless of all the mistakes, so they could shape me and prepare me for what came next.

I don't believe God was punishing me. And he was faithful to meet me and teach me. He never left me to figure out where to go on my own. He comforted me, deepened my trust in him, and revealed to me the places where I needed to grow. I'll never know how things might have gone if I hadn't made the choices I made. But what I do know is that he never failed me or anyone else.

Your story may or may not be similar to mine, but one thing we will always have in common is that no story is ever too messed up for us to do the next right thing. Every day you live, you wake up to new mercies, new opportunities to learn from your failures, and new chances to keep growing into a better version of yourself.

The same God who never left Joseph, even when circumstances seemed hopeless, is the same God who will never stop healing, teaching, restoring, and redeeming us. When people get it wrong—when we get it wrong—we have a Father who keeps meeting us in the dark, keeps shining light on our path, and relentlessly pursues his dreams for us and for the world by weaving together the good with the not so good, the beautiful with the messy, the past with the future.

## Chapter Twelve

# ROGUE, NOT REBELLIOUS

Have you ever felt like you just didn't fit in? Junior high doesn't count; we all feel that way in junior high. But I'm talking about in real life and in your own skin. Like you're playing a role that you realize isn't really you?

That was me for a long time. I especially felt like that throughout those last few years of The Crux after the "planting" part was over and we had entered the "tending" and "pruning" phase.

There wasn't anything wrong with the people. They were amazing. I genuinely loved them. I just felt caged up inside, like I had become someone I always feared I would become. But I didn't know why I felt so lost.

Was I afraid of serving God? No. I had gotten over that. I knew his heart and character at a greater capacity than I ever had before. This feeling was something deeper, more primal.

During that time, I didn't have much peace, and I was looking for it in all kinds of places. So when I'm unsure in life or I sense that something is lacking, I become a self-help junkie. At least that's what my counselor tells me, and she is right. Dang it—she's always right.

When I'm on a self-help bender, I read. A lot. Which is sort of weird because I struggled to read when I was a kid. I vividly remember the first book I ever actually finished was *Where the Red Fern Grows* and I was in fifth grade. I can remember sitting on the couch in our living room, crying embarrassingly hard. Dog stories still have that effect on me. But over time I developed a love for reading and for discovering my way into breakthroughs.

I'm not sure how I found the book *Houses That Change the World* by Wolfgang Simson. I had never really heard of house churches or the history of how they changed the world...but change the world they did!

When I was getting my degree in Christian ministries, either I slept through the class where they covered this part of church history, or they never taught it. But I consumed the book's pages like oxygen. The risks these rogue pioneering Christians took in order to meet together as followers of Jesus were astounding!

Did you know it was illegal to even have a church building the first three hundred years of Christianity? Crazy, huh? These stories connected to something that had been lying dormant in my soul. These stories awakened part of me to life and reminded me of the plot line of a movie I wished I could star in. During this time in my life when I wasn't feeling right in my own skin, reading these stories called out to my longing for adventure and the advancement of God's mission in the world. This was something I'd been missing.

Then I discovered *The Forgotten Ways* by Alan Hirsch. This book opened my mind and connected with my soul as I learned more about the history of the world-changing expansion of the church. I read about how the early church was led by men and women who were living out their passionate love for Jesus through their God-given design, and I began to realize what was missing in my life. Their ways of building a ministry were just not things I had forgotten—I was never told they existed!

These books revealed to me that what I had always assumed was an obedience problem was actually an imagination problem. I think this is true for most of us. It's not that we wouldn't follow Jesus where he wants to lead us. It's that we can't actually imagine where he's leading. We have a deficit of imagination. Maybe it's because of the culture we grew up in, or maybe we didn't have visionaries and dreamers around us. Maybe no one ever gave us permission to do things differently than the way it had always been done. The reason for the deficit doesn't really matter. The dangerous problem is the deficit itself. The good news is that God has the remedy in Jeremiah 33:3:

> This is God's Message, the God who made earth, made it livable and lasting, known everywhere as God: "Call to me and I will answer you. I'll tell you marvelous and wondrous things that you could never figure out on your own."

What an invitation. He is asking us to call on him. He is promising us that he will tell us "marvelous and wondrous things"! I mean, how awesome is that?

If you currently feel like you don't fit or your life doesn't make sense, I'm pretty sure there is nothing wrong with you either. Maybe everything that is right about you just needs to be discovered. Taking God at his word and calling on him is how he asks us to discover these things we simply can not figure out on our own. Sometimes the answer to our prayers happens in conversations with old friends about new discoveries about bees.

Well, that's how it happened for me. One influential day my friend Micah, who personally understood my lack of imagination and inward struggle, sat me down and began to explain the inner workings of beehives, more specifically, the role of rogue bees. I had never heard of rogue bees before, but I learned that they are the research and development arm of the bee kingdom.

In any given beehive, more than 90 percent of the bees are worker bees. They have a crucial role to play, which is to maintain the health and vitality of the beehive and help produce life-giving honey. These bees perform what's called the waggle dance to communicate to each other where to find the pollen.

But inside every hive, there are approximately seven to nine rogue bees who ignore the waggle dance and respond to the deeper rhythm of their "beeing"—sorry, pun intended. These rogue bees in a sense dance to their own beat in search of pollen rather than conforming to the waggle of the other bees.

These bees have been studied for years, and their methods have perplexed scientists. It seemed that the rogue bees had no direction in their seemingly random adventures. Some researchers assumed the rogue bees just stumbled around haphazardly, out of sync with the rest of the hive. But eventually researchers realized that the actions of the rogue bees were paramount to the longevity of the hive. Without them, the hive would become so efficient at exploiting the known food locations that the bees would end up consuming it all and the hive would die out. Basically, without the rogues, the rest of the bees would eat themselves to death. These bees aren't rebellious or counterproductive. They serve an essential purpose by not doing what all the other bees do. And, unfortunately, the rogues often die in the process of saving the hive.

I know this bee story may sound random to some people, but for me, it was like a lightbulb went off. For the first time in my life I realized that I wasn't a rebel. I was a rogue. This discovery changed my life. I can't adequately describe to you the peace I experienced when I realized that all this time I hadn't been resisting God or his calling on my life. I just couldn't rest until I found it. For so many years I believed the lie that I was a terrible pastor. I didn't love people well. I would ask myself, *Why can't you just settle down and be happy?* The lies and attacks against my identity were constant. My missional freak-out about not having any influential relationships with anybody who didn't already know Jesus totally made sense, looking back.

I was created to be sent out to find new opportunities. I was designed to create and find the future. Imagine the joy when I realized that Jesus was a rogue, too, sent to come and find lost sheep and pioneer the New Covenant.

Every one of the dreams I had pursued to this point now made sense. Yes I wanted to be a rock star and had the ability to play drums, but the thing that drew me most to this vision wasn't just performing music and playing drums. What I loved so much about Stryper and U2 was that they took amazing music and showmanship and, in a covert, somewhat undercover, pioneering way, made a huge impact in the lives of people who were not yet seeking God.

My lack of maturity and underdeveloped character drew me to people like Tommy Lee from Mötley Crüe. Rogues can easily become rebellious if they don't understand who God has created us to be or how he is inviting them to join him in creating the future. A frustrated rogue may just want to get drunk and destroy a hotel room, or land a helicopter on someone's front yard.

Maybe someday Tommy Lee will learn that he is a rogue, too, not a rebel. Maybe there's still a chance we will rock out together after all.

I'm so thankful that, upon my exit from The Crux, there were people who embraced me and my rogue pioneering apostolic spirit. Every decision from that point on in my life was made with this understanding of myself, and I no longer feel like I'm living someone else's dream or that there is something wrong with me.

I don't want you to waste another moment of your life thinking there's something wrong with you. God not only puts dreams inside us, but he custom designs us to fulfill those dreams. Don't waste another day playing someone else's role in the story of your life.

## Chapter Thirteen
# WOVEN, NOT WASTED

I n the life cycle of a dream, the birth is exciting, living in pursuit of it is exhilarating, and its death is devastating. But the resurrection is worth it all. When I felt free to be me and follow the kind of dreams I was created to live out, I began to see how all the threads of my life—my identity, my love for music, my experiences, even my mistakes—had been miraculously woven together, moment by moment. Every thread counted. Nothing was wasted. Everything that had ever been woven into my story would always remain part of me.

Just like the elaborately woven multicolored coat Joseph's father gave to him, God weaves together our experiences, personalities, abilities, and uniqueness to create a sort of Technicolor dream coat designed to fit us perfectly. And it felt amazing.

My experience in Bosnia would eventually give birth to new dreams, which would lead me out of church ministry and into adventures that suited me and my gifts and passions better than

I could have ever hoped. While doing those experimental events at local bars, connecting with people where they were already gathering, a seed had been planted that would grow into a nonprofit called Blackbird Mission. With the encouragement of my friend Johnny, who was a tremendous cheerleader and collaborator, I would dream up new ways of reaching people in the everyday spaces and places of life. Everyone needs a friend like Johnny who gets excited with you and can see a glimpse of what you're seeing when no one else can see it yet. He was instrumental in naming Blackbird Mission and helping me getting if off the ground.

Even the *Weekend at Bernie's* version of Paradigm 5 served as a testing ground for an idea that would end up growing into a weekly venture called Pub Theology, which became the first mission we launched through Blackbird. In those early days, we needed a person of peace at a local bar who could help create an environment where we could get the idea off the ground. Then one night during a gig at Joe's 2 bar, a worship leader named Aaron walked in from a megachurch in town. We knew each other, and he was aware that I was in a transitional season of life. That night he mentioned to me that he thought I should meet his boss and that his church might be a place that could get behind an idea like Pub Theology.

I did go meet that pastor. He was a person of peace. It was a church of peace. In fact, you'll love this: While interviewing with that church, I was open and honest with the executive pastor about the circumstances surrounding my departure from The Crux. I let him know that my ministry credentials were revoked because I had consumed alcohol against my denomination's policy. He said he wanted to hear the whole story and recommended that we sit down and talk about it over some top-shelf bourbon at his house. I thought maybe I was being punked for a hidden camera show, but he was for real.

The staff welcomed me. They hired me. They believed in me. They also restored my standing as a pastor with the privilege to speak on a regular basis in their church. It was a crazy huge, dysfunctional megachurch, but it became a place of shelter for my family and myself at a time when we needed that. Often after a dream dies we need a place of shelter and peace. If you have just walked through the death of a dream, ask God for a place of peace and a space of shelter. He can provide.

While on staff there, I created a "rogue bee" research and development arm of the church that would help us reach the surrounding community through Pub Theology events. After the Paradigm 5 guys had gone their separate ways, Damon and I remained in Indy. We, along with Johnny, put together a great band we called The Travellers, and the Pub Theology concept began to build momentum. We started playing three-hour gigs at local bars, and at the end of the night, in between "Knocking on Heaven's Door" by Bob Dylan and "Hallelujah" by Leonard Cohen, I would share a brief thought of the night. Each talk was only about three minutes and was a simple reflection about faith, hope, love, or forgiveness before we closed with our final song.

The atmosphere of the bar changed during those final moments. After the set, people wanted to talk about the things they were going through. They talked to us about people they needed to forgive. They longed to know they were loved unconditionally. And I felt an important shift happening. Rather than inviting God into my dreams, I felt that God was letting me be part of *his* dream.

After one particular Saturday night gig, Johnny and I were talking with the bar's general manager, Jimmy. We shared with him our vision for Pub Theology and for doing gigs like these more often. I always loved Jimmy's heart. He was not a believer at the time, and I knew he had fought a lot of his own demons over the years. But he said he would think about it. We finished the gig, tore down and loaded all the gear, and as usual with these gigs got home after two a.m.

I finally lay down in my bed around three o'clock in the morning and then woke up early to speak at all three services at the megachurch the next morning. Operating on very little sleep, I was beyond shocked to see Jimmy walk in and sit about halfway back in the front section. Church was not something Jimmy did. Ever.

After the service, I received a text from him that said, "Daron, I don't know what just happened? I don't know what made me feel like I just did? That was amazing. Thank you for this and PUB THEOLOGY IS GOING TO HAPPEN!!!!" In all caps, just like that.

Jimmy went to bat for us with the owner of the bar, and within a few months in the spring of 2009 we hosted our first official Pub Theology event with the tagline "Indy's best party with a purpose." Jimmy's influence opened the doors for Pub Theology, and in the process, his life was dramatically impacted by the unconditional love of God that we talked about and tried our best to live out each week.

As Pub Theology was starting to get off the ground and I was in the process of getting the word out around town, I distributed flyers printed with the details of our next few events. On the front of the flier was our logo and big letters that read: "Pub Theology: Faith, Hope, Love and Beer." If that sounds a little bit controversial, that was the goal. I wanted to choose a tagline that brought together four words that neither religious nor nonreligious people thought could go together. I knew the flyer might offend some religious people—like those who came from my previous church affiliation—but I also hoped, and ended up proving over the course of ten years, that nonreligious people were curious about how those words might relate to them.

Week after week I was blown away to discover the way Jesus still transforms adults. He is still healing people and drawing them in. I finally understood how the missional freakout I experienced wasn't because Jesus was unfaithful; it was because *I* was! When I got outside the walls of the church and into those everyday spaces and places of life, I realized that I didn't take Jesus there. He had been there the whole time.

A man name Stu came to the bar one night during the Christmas season. He was making his way to a couple of office Christmas parties, and a coworker brought him to Pub Theology to end the night with us. That night I shared the story of the first Christmas and what an absolute mess that night must have been. I don't think most of us would have actually wanted to be there. If you have kids, maybe you were nervous about the delivery of your first child even in the most sanitary conditions. I remember how nervous I was transporting my pregnant wife in a safe car with at least eight working airbags. Yet Mary and Joseph took their long journey on a donkey and delivered Jesus in a stable they shared with farm animals. Evidently God forgot to call ahead and get reservations for his own son? I went on to share that if this was the chaotic, unclean, humble, and vulnerable way that Jesus showed up on the earth, there was probably no mess in your life that God couldn't enter into as well.

That night Stu walked up to me, tears streaming down his face, and said, "I never thought it could be true! I never thought that God could love me with my drinks and my smokes. But now I know that he's here and that he loves me. Thank you. Merry Christmas."

It was moments like these I always hoped and imagined might be possible. And they happened over and over again. Hundreds of people were surprised to learn that they were loved, right where they were. I came to realize over and over again that nothing is ever wasted; it is all woven.

It was Pub Theology that finally gave me the opportunity to use my all gifts and step fully into who I was created to be. So many threads! I had the joy of leading and setting vision for the organization, teaching and playing drums at events, and hosting follow-up groups that helped me reach people with the life-giving truth that God's Love is always accessible and relevant to our daily lives. For more than ten years we held weekly events in bars across the city, and then hosted follow-up conversations and spiritual mentoring groups at each of the bars.

I would love to tell you story after story of people who met Jesus in these bars. I would tell you about Kat, Rich, Megan, Michelle, Nick, Jamie, Mindi, Anna, and Emily. The list goes on and on. Their stories read like modern day miracles. I would love to write another book filled with their stories.

Their stories, these bars, our conversations, the baptisms prove that hope is still alive, and they changed my life forever. I loved every minute of it. *Wow.* What a life. What a dream. What a God! Stepping out to create Pub Theology was just the first of many more threads that would be woven together and would allow me to become part of new dreams God was putting together and inviting me into.

I would come to understand better over time how, throughout my life, I always had the heart of a pioneer. The fancy biblical word for this quality is *apostolic*. I didn't see it for so long, but it was that apostolic heart for innovation that had always fueled my passion for creating and leading unique spiritual experiences. And as I grew to understand more about what this calling means, I dedicated my life to pursuing the types of dreams that fit the apostolic gift that was woven into my spiritual DNA. In time, I would created a process for other people to understand their own spiritual DNA, so they could understand how their dreams are connected to their natural gifts, personality, and passions.

In September 2012, I left the megachurch to run Blackbird Mission full-time. I no longer felt the need to resurrect the third grade version of the dream, or the college student version, or even the "Pastor Daron" version. I would come to understand that none of those versions of the dream—or the lessons that came from them—were wasted.

Pursuing my rock and roll dreams was simply a thread being woven into a bigger story. Not a moment of that time was wasted. All the miles traveled, all those bar gigs with Paradigm 5, the massive disappointment at the Whisky A Go Go were woven, not wasted. Even a terrifying night in Michigan when our van was locked in a cage while we performed and watching the bartender sell drugs and people get high all night...woven, not wasted. The countless camps and conferences...woven, not wasted. The years invested in creating a unique faith community at The Crux and even learning what *doesn't* fit...woven, not wasted. Even the missional freak-out that led me to get kicked out of my denomination...woven, not wasted.

All your life experiences from as far back as you can remember are threads that may not have made sense at the time, but together they came together to prepare you for what is yet to come. That childhood business you started? It's in there. That time you ran for student council president because you really wanted to make a difference? It's in there. The discipline required to play on that state championship team in high school in hopes of getting signed to the pros or at least a scholarship to college? It's all woven in there. The confusing parts, the choices you thought were best at the time but you're still paying for, every tear you've cried, and the worst mistakes you've ever made? Every one of those things just add to the strength, resilience, color, and texture of the masterpiece being woven into the fiber of your life.

The same is true for all of us. The wins and the losses. The joy and the pain. The victories and defeats. The things we feel we did in vain. The things that changed us forever, and even things we thought would change everything and turned out to be disappointments. None of it is ever wasted.

One thread I had almost forgotten about became important as I continued to follow my heart and natural leadership style. Did your high school have morning announcements right at the beginning of first period? I remember a voice on the intercom being broadcast into homerooms across the school. Each morning the voice led us in the Pledge of Allegiance and delivered the morning announcements. Most schools' principals or vice principals did the morning announcements, but at Tempe High School the announcements were done by students. For most students, morning announcements were not a big deal. But in my head, I viewed it like a really short morning radio show. I would listen to the people doing the announcements, then imagine what I would do differently if the microphone was in front of me.

For the first three years of high school, I imagined cueing the mic and doing it better, funnier, or more exciting. Then, at last, my senior year arrived, and I tried out to for the part of delivering our school's morning announcements. After planning it all in my head for years, I finally got the gig. And I loved every morning of it.

Up until I started doing morning announcements, I was kind of self-conscious about my voice. It had become increasingly deeper throughout high school, and I thought it sounded weird. But I pushed through the self-conscious fear, and I'm glad I did. Side note: Fear is your enemy, and it's almost always a liar.

Inspired by the Robin Williams movie *Good Morning, Vietnam*, I started every morning with a hearty *"Gooooooooood moooooooooorrrrrnnnnning, Tempe High!"* I loved it, the students loved it, and most of the teachers hated it (but the latter were incorrect—it was awesome).

At the close of my senior year I received an award for excellence in doing the announcements. That whole year people kept telling me that I should get into radio and would ask if I'd thought about it before. I hadn't thought seriously about it, but I think that's because I didn't have the imagination at that point to consider how radio could be part of my calling. Or maybe I was so laser-focused on the music part of my dream that I didn't even consider any other possibilities. At that point I had no idea how that experience, too, would be a thread. Moments that were not wasted, but woven into my story long before it made any sense.

Einstein said, "Imagination is more important than knowledge." This was a guy who had way more knowledge swimming around in his head than most, so that's an observation worth taking to heart.

In the thousands of conversations I've had with people over the years, that lack of imagination I mentioned is possibly one of the greatest barriers keeping many of us from becoming who we were born to be. Most of us do not have an imagination big enough for what God can do. Maybe it's what you believe about yourself or what you believe about God, probably a combination of both, but there's one thing I know: God specializes in doing exceedingly more than we can ask or imagine.

Completing the life cycle of your dreams means asking him to expand your imagination. I tell you this because that's what kept happening in my story, and I want you to experience this, too. It happened when I stopped trying to create the end results of my micro story and started trusting the unforced rhythms of grace Jesus has invited us into whenever we're ready and willing.

Ok back to this next crazy God dream thread story. In 2009, we were gaining some momentum with Pub Theology, and one Monday morning I was driving my oldest son to kindergarten while listening to the number one pop radio station in Indianapolis, 99.5 WZPL. The Smiley Morning Show, hosted by Dave Smiley, was playing. Dave was a little crazy, unscripted, really funny, and relatable. He was also a pastor's kid, which always sort of endeared me to him. And on that particular morning, he was doing a remote podcast at a breakfast spot right around the corner from our house.

I eyed one singular Pub Theology flyer on the floor of the car, then the thought jumped into my brain: "You need to go deliver this flyer to Smiley!" So we drove to the restaurant and walked in. The hostess asked if we needed a table, and I told her we were just there to give this flyer to the DJ.

Then the hostess had a genius idea: "You should have your son give it to him."

Brilliant. Who could say no to a cute kid? So I handed Cole the flyer, and he walked it over to Dave. At this point, Dave was live on the air. He looked over at Cole and said, "Hey, little buddy, do you want an autograph?"

I motioned to Smiley that he was just handing him the flyer. He proceeds to read it live on the air. "Pub Theology: Faith, Hope, Love, and Beer! This sounds like a church for me!"

At this point, I'm thinking this is going amazingly well. Then Smiley says, "Grab a seat, dude. Tell me what Pub Theology is all about." I sit down, live on the air, and explain the heart behind Pub Theology. "I've been a pastor for a long time. I'm also a pastor's kid. I am tired of saying the same things to most of the same people every week. I want to create an environment where people in the everyday spaces and places of life can be reminded, or maybe told for the first time, that God loves them."

Smiley thought it was cool and even said he might check out a Pub Theology event sometime. Needless to say, we were late getting my son to kindergarten that day. I remember thinking there was no way Smiley would actually show up, but I considered being able to talk about it live on WZPL a win.

Imagine my surprise when Smiley walked into the next Pub Theology event. He made frequent visits after that, too, and even showed up at church when I spoke. We developed a friendship over the years, and his journey with Jesus continues to this day. It's complicated and a little messy, just like mine…and maybe like yours, too.

One day when we were having lunch together, Smiley said, "Hey, why don't you come in and let me interview you on my show again about Pub Theology?" I jumped at the chance, of course, but then we began to imagine ways this could become more than a onetime interview.

We came up with the idea of bringing back a segment of his show he used to call Therapy Thursday, during which I would come in as Pastor Daron every Thursday to take listeners' calls and do my best to give them sound biblical advice. This wasn't always easy. If you take much time to listen to popular morning drive-time radio shows, you know that the comedy and the comments are not typically church friendly. But I realized I could either get offended or I could get invited. I've learned that when we choose to get defensive every time someone says something we don't agree with, we might make our point, but we will most likely not make a connection. This is a value that I believe Jesus modeled, and it motivated so much of the work we did with Pub Theology.

Just think of how often Jesus could've gotten offended on a daily basis. He literally is God in the flesh hanging out with prostitutes, thieves, and drunks. Yet we don't read a single instance where Jesus stomped out of a party, offended by a joke or an offhand comment someone made. He stayed in the room with people. He showed everyone that his love was greater than his personal piety.

So I showed up as a guest on the Smiley Morning Show every Therapy Thursday for a couple of years. As I was leaving the station one day, the program director, J.R., pulled me aside and asked if I ever thought about hosting my own show on WZPL.

I prayed about it for about a nanosecond and replied, "Yes, I have!" It's important to note that my only actual training for this came back in high school, when I did morning announcements at Tempe High School. Call it courage or stupidity, but I was all about this opportunity to expand the reach of our message. In spite of my lack of experience, I was in fact very prepared. All those years standing on all those stages answering all those questions at Pub Theology had prepared me for hosting a three-hour Sunday morning drive-time radio show, which we called Radio Theology.

Everything I learned through Pub Theology was again being woven into the next dream God was inviting me into. I absolutely loved everything about hosting Radio Theology. The potential of connecting with over a million listeners every Sunday morning, the opportunity to talk about Jesus on the number one secular pop station in my city, and talking about faith and hope and love in between Justin Bieber and Ariana Grande songs was an opportunity I could never have imagined back when I was playing youth camps or trying to plant a church. The music, interviewing the artists, the communication, the outreach, the comedy, the absolute fun—every part of it brought together threads that had been there my whole life.

One night I was invited to hang out with Jon Bellion on his tour bus after a concert. He talked about his deep love for Jesus and how he was trying to live out that faith in the music industry. I'll never forget that conversation, talking about the prophetic soul in his lyrics and the encouragement he received from other artists to stay out of the contemporary Christian genre so his music could keep reaching broader audiences.

When I look at how Jesus wove the threads of my life together, I don't know whether to laugh at the absurdity of it all or cry for ever mistrusting God's heart and vision for my life. We really are the workmanship of God created in Christ Jesus to do good works that he prepared in advance for us to do. Nothing is wasted. It is all woven together to create the dreams on his heart for our joy and for his eternal purposes.

I hosted Radio Theology for the next three and a half years and started having visions of us syndicating the show and taking it nationwide. We even started having conversations with people in the radio industry about it. Then 2020 happened. As COVID-19 spread across the world, killing well over four million people, I was grateful to survive the virus physically (although it was a rough couple of weeks), but the virus also killed a lot of dreams.

Initially, Radio Theology was put on ninety-day life support during the months when businesses were locking down because of the international pandemic. The radio station furloughed most of its employees and DJs. But after those initial ninety days, the station was still not hiring part-time staff or DJs, and no one was even allowed to enter the building. So Radio Theology had to end. Even as I write these words, it is still dead in the water. But were those three and a half years wasted? Not a chance!

I can't wait to see how these experiences will be woven into the future. How will this dream be resurrected? No idea. I just know that I don't have to force anything. His ways are higher than mine. I finally believe that. Will it look like it once did? Probably not. Am I okay with that? Yup! Will it be with the same team? On the same station? In the same time slot? I'm guessing it won't.

I did let myself grieve during a brief summer pity party that we'll call my own personal memorial service for Radio Theology. Then I let it die. I took everything I knew to be true about God's heart and his dreams for me and I pivoted.

We took everything the radio show had taught us and pivoted toward purpose. That pivot toward purpose launched the Daron Earlewine Podcast, which I now host every week. It is available not just on syndicated radio stations but all over the world. Every week on the podcast, I remind people of three important truths that the threads in my life have revealed. First, God created each of us on purpose and for a purpose, so he will be faithful to open opportunities for us to give our best back to him. Second, he is for us and always working ahead of us to create opportunities that he has been preparing for us to step into since long before we were born. And finally, he is always near us, never far away in this process. He promised not to leave us or forsake us, so we can remain yoked with him for life. Wherever he leads, we can follow with confidence as we have watched him weave together the threads for a future yet to be created.

None of us knows what the next chapter of our mission will look like, but God does. He knows better than any of us what our world needs from us most. You make sense. You have a unique spiritual DNA that fits into a huge masterpiece that God prepared in advance for you and for this world he loves so much. As you're walking around on this planet—even with dreams that have seemingly breathed their last—just know that what you *can't* see right now is far bigger than what you *can* see.

If you're tired of hearing me say that everything—and I mean *everything*—is woven, not wasted, then I'll stop now. But I hope you will look at all the threads and loose ends in your life that feel random and messy and know that you are no accident. Not even your accidents can change that.

*Chapter Fourteen*

# THE WEIGHT OF YOUR CALLING

You're blessed when you've worked up a good appetite for God. He's food and drink in the best meal you'll ever eat.

—*Matthew 5:6*

So the last time we checked in with Joseph, he was still in prison. Unlike us, Joseph didn't have a copy of The Message to crack open to recount God's faithfulness through the ages, even when everything looked hopeless for an innocent man sitting in prison.

While there aren't many things I would dislike more than the death of a dream during an Indiana sleet storm, prison would definitely be at the top of that list. Yet, even as Joseph sat in prison, God was at work in the meanwhile, just as he always is. Pharaoh had a dream that he was standing on the bank of the Nile River, and in his dream he saw seven fat, healthy cows come up out of the river and begin grazing in the grass by a marsh. Then he saw seven more cows come up behind them from the river, but they were scrawny and thin. The skinny cows came up beside the fat cows on the riverbank, then the scrawny cows ate the healthy cows. How's that for a disturbing dream?

At that point in the dream, Pharaoh woke up. He knew there had to be a message in it for him, but he had no clue what that message might be. He needed someone to interpret the dream, so he reached out to all the magicians and wise men he had access to as king of Egypt. Not one of them could tell him what the dream meant.

Then, finally, the king's cupbearer spoke up. The cupbearer, by the way, was a trusted member of the king's inner circle, whose job it was to drink from the king's cup before he did to make sure the drink wasn't poisoned. If the cupbearer died after taking a sip, the king would know not to take a drink. So...not exactly a dream job for anyone who wasn't loyal.

The cupbearer told Pharaoh about the dream he had years earlier in prison and about Joseph's accurate interpretation. Pharaoh immediately sent for Joseph and recounted the dream to him. After hearing the details of the dream, Joseph's next words revealed the character development that happened during his season in prison: "It is beyond my power to do this...But God can tell you what it means and set you at ease" (Genesis 41:16 NLT).

Do you remember the young, arrogant version of Joseph at the start of this story? He had ambition but no filter. He arrogantly spouted off about how awesome he was going to be. I imagine him as an ancient version of Muhammad Ali in his prime, telling everybody he was the greatest. But we don't pick up an ounce of that arrogance in this more mature version of Joseph. When given a fresh opportunity to use his gifts and abilities, he didn't take credit.

Joseph went on to interpret Pharoah's dream. It was a weighty message that would impact the entire nation of Egypt. The seven healthy cows represented seven years of abundance, and the weak cows represented seven years of famine. He explained that a famine would coming to the land, and if Pharaoh didn't prepare for it, the nation would be doomed. The nation would have seven years of abundance to prepare for the famine. God would provide what they needed in advance, but the nation would have to prepare.

Pharaoh not only released Joseph from his prison sentence, but effective immediately, he promoted him to a high position where he would help the entire nation of Egypt prepare for this famine. This story gets better and better, and we read in Genesis 41:39–44:

> So Pharaoh said to Joseph, "You're the man for us. God has given you the inside story—no one is as qualified as you in experience and wisdom. From now on, you're in charge of my affairs; all my people will report to you..."
>
> So Pharaoh commissioned Joseph: "I'm putting you in charge of the entire country of Egypt." Then Pharaoh removed his signet ring from his finger and slipped it on Joseph's hand. He outfitted him in robes of the best linen and

> put a gold chain around his neck. He put the second-in-command chariot at his disposal, and as he rode people shouted "Bravo!"
>
> ...Pharaoh told Joseph, "I am Pharaoh, but no one in Egypt will make a single move without your stamp of approval."

Joseph had dreamed about this day since years earslier when he was just the annoying kid brother trying to prove to his brothers that God had big plans for him. God's spirit was with him, inviting him into his dreams. But God couldn't work his plan without Joseph doing his part.

Joseph was elevated and given authority, and he met his responsibilities with wisdom and courage over the next seven years. He prepared Egypt for the coming famine, helping organize grain reserves and managing resources that would keep the nation going strong. As a result, people from all around the world came to Egypt to buy grain from Joseph, because the famine was impacting other regions of the world, too.

When big opportunities presented themselves, Joseph had the strength of character to do what was required. During his years in prison, I believe Joseph's character was being developed not just *in spite* of his circumstances, but *because* of his circumstances.

Maturity didn't just benefit him vocationally. It also impacted his future, his relationships, his family, his nation, and the generations that would follow him. The same is true for us. Our calling is bigger than our vocation. We are called as parents, spouses, neighbors, and human beings to carry ourselves in a manner that accomplishes God's purposes in every area of lives.

Your calling and journey will be different from Joseph's, but the reality is the same. The degree to which you are able to fulfill God's dreams—for you and for the world—will always be directly related to your character. The person you are in the dark, when no one is watching, is where the foundation of strong character is poured.

Joseph chose humility, courage, gratitude, and faithfulness. These are the four foundational character traits that keep us all from going off the rails. These are the four things I constantly aspire to and pray for. Every night, as I put my three boys to bed, these are the characteristics I pray they will develop. I pray the same for you.

## Humility

We don't have to experience failure, betrayal, or a wrongful prison sentence to choose humility. In fact, I vote "no, thank you" on prison for all of us. But even prison presented Joseph with the opportunity to choose humility. He could have been a real jerk when he was brought out of prison to interpret Pharoah's dream. Instead, he took the chance to acknowledge that it was God alone who could give him the insight to interpret Pharoah's dream. Then, he was humble enough to say yes to the opportunity he was given, even when he had no idea that opportunity would allow him to be freed from prison and promoted to the highest-ranking position in the Egyptian government. It is very possible that it was his humility, not his ability to interpret the dream, that ultimately found Joseph in the position to which he was promoted.

Humility reminds us that our dreams are never about us. I've heard it said that humility isn't necessarily thinking less of yourself. It's thinking of yourself less. Humility reminds us of who we really are: imperfect beings made from particles of earth who are also given access to the very Spirit of God to empower us to live as forces of good in this world.

## Courage

It may have been Joseph's humility that prepared him, but it was his courage that helped him seize the moment. Courage could also be understood as *heart*. It is often said that courage is not the absence of fear, but the presence of faith. If you are going to seize each day God has prepared for you, like Joseph, you will need courage.

Throughout Scripture, it's clear that God is pretty hyped on courage. So many Old Testament stories tell us how God journeyed with his people, time and again, providing for them and reminding them to be strong and courageous. In the New Testament, anytime humans encountered an angelic being, they were told the same thing: "Do not be afraid. Take courage."

How do we develop courage? We recognize that fear usually lies to us. We do small things every day that scare us just a little. Because courage is a daily choice. If we are waiting for our fears to subside, we will wait forever. Before we take a risk, before we obey, before we can keep moving toward our calling, it's easy to think our fear will eventually subside. We can waste a lot of time fearing the outcomes of our decisions and never actually move forward. Fortunately, we are not called to manage outcomes. We don't have that kind of control. We are just called to obedience, which always requires courage.

## Gratitude

Choosing humility and courageous obedience not only *requires* gratitude, but it *multiplies* gratitude. And gratitude is the pathway to joy and wholeness. Gratitude has become an important value to me and, in turn, to my family over the years. Julie and I now ask our sons at the end of every day to recount something they are grateful for. They are learning the power of gratitude while they are young. Our hope is that gratitude becomes a habit ingrained in their hearts to help build their character for their own callings.

Gratitude even helps us reframe failures and memories of the past, bring us into the present moment, and prepare us to create the future. Even if in seasons of struggle, pain, or failure, if you can find simple gratitude, you've got a solid starting point to reclaim your sense of hope and joy.

How do we grow in gratitude? We start small. Every day, start and finish your day with simple gratitude. Notice the taste of food, the smell of flowers, or the ability to walk. Express gratitude for music, a smile, or a sunrise.

I urge you to give it a shot and see what a difference it makes in your outlook. When you focus on growing more grateful about little things, over time you will notice your perspective about bigger things also shifts. Try it and see if it doesn't help strengthen you and propel you.

## Faithfulness

Faithfulness is simply doing what needs to be done, even when you don't feel like doing it. And it isn't really about just doing tasks; it's about being faithful to the people in your life. Joseph had been faithful to Potipher, whether or not anyone realized that or believed him. And the reason the cupbearer remembered him was a testament to his faithfulness long before he stood before Pharaoh. He was faithful when no one noticed. But eventually his faithfulness was recognized.

While Joseph sat in prison, there had to have been so many times when he felt that his faithfulness didn't matter. But he humbly and courageously remained faithful. He would discover that it was his faithfulness that brought him back into the palace, and it was that same foundation that deepened his ability to handle the weight of his new position. His faithfulness in prison trained him for the power and authority he would take on in the palace.

If you are wise and faithful now, you will be amazed at the way you invite blessing in the future. The fancy biblical word for faithfulness is *sanctification*, which simply means being set apart as someone whose internal character holds up when everything else seems to be going wrong. Joseph's story exemplifies for us a story of sanctification instead of sabotage.

I wonder how Joseph's story and the future of Egypt might have gone if he had chosen to become bitter instead of humble. What if he hadn't chosen courage and put himself out there again, even after his last position landed him in prison for no reason? When his dreams died with his brothers' betrayal, what if he had chosen the road of self-pity and took on a victim mentality? What if he had chosen ingratitude and allowed his ego take over? That's how it could have gone, and sadly, I think that's often how it goes when we face the pain of life.

If Joseph had chosen not to continuously work on building his character, what might have happened to the people across the nation during the famine? God would have had to call on someone else to save and redeem his people. We don't know how or who he would have partnered with to accomplish it. We just know it probably wouldn't have been Joseph.

You're probably not in Egypt, and maybe there's not an actual famine where you are, but in your city, your school, your neighborhood, and your family, spiritual famine is always present. The words of Jesus and the life he modeled is a guide that brings light in the darkness. That is always going to be part of our calling—to carry that light to the world. And he promised that he will be with us always in this mission, even to the very end of the age.

Scripture reminds us again and again that God is saving and redeeming this world. Will you be yoked with him when he does? I don't want you to miss out on the thrill of life with him. Embrace character transformation as passionately as you pursue your dreams. When you do, the world will be more filled with faith, hope, and love as a result—and *you* will be filled with them, too.

*Chapter Fifteen*

# FORGIVENESS

You're blessed when you get your inside world—your mind and heart—put right. Then you can see God in the outside world. You're blessed when you can show people how to cooperate instead of compete or fight. That's when you discover who you really are, and your place in God's family.

—*Matthew 5:8–9*

One of the greatest obstacles to maturing into the weight of our calling is forgiveness. No matter what we have gone through and no matter what we have done to ourselves, there comes a moment when we have to make a very difficult decision. Are we going to choose forgiveness—for ourselves and for others?

Honestly, this is a decision we will have to keep making over and over again. Forgiving is not a onetime decision. To live in a spirit of forgiveness, way down to our depths, we have to keep forgiving. That is the only way our hearts can become whole and healed without constantly reinjuring ourselves.

Healing can take days, months, or, in many cases, years. This is a journey that often requires counseling and some deep, difficult inner work. The good news is that it is so worth it! And it's absolutely necessary if you are ever going to experience the resurrection of your dreams and become the person you were always meant be.

Years after everything went down with the band and the dream died, one day there came a knock on my front door. When I opened the door, there stood Lee. He had traveled back to Indiana for a business meeting, but carved out some time out to find me, sit down face-to-face, and ask for forgiveness.

It was a humble and courageous decision that meant a lot to me. Together Lee and I sat on my back porch and talked about our memories and all the good times we had experienced. We also discussed the tough times. He gave me some perspective about what he had been going through during that time and those seasons and where God had led him. He asked for forgiveness again. I gave it again. But the reality is, I had already forgiven Lee.

It started when we were in counseling as a band. Those sessions helped us talk through the process of forgiveness and its importance if we are ever going to experience the freedom and power it gives us. I know I forgave him before we got together to open for Delirious?, but as we sat on my back deck that afternoon, I forgave him again. And I meant it. I meant it every time. I think that's the tricky thing about forgiveness. You have to come to a moment when you choose to do it, but then you often have to keep reminding yourself to live in that space.

"Oh yeah, they are forgiven" we have to keep reminding ourselves. "I have canceled the debt they owe me. I forgive them...still."

If I'm honest, sometimes it was just easier to blame Lee than it was to trust God. I think that in those first years, while I was tending to the soil of my soul, I had to keep weeding out the bitterness that constantly tried to take root.

In the moments when I was reminded that I wasn't living the dream I wanted, I could reach down and grab a handful of anger out of my heart and sit in a stew of "life's not fair" with a side of "this wasn't the life I was supposed to live."

Those thoughts often happened for me when I attended a concert. They almost always happened when I saw a tour bus. I have a weird obsession with tour buses. I can remember watching videos on MTV, back when they played videos, and there were all these cool slow-motion scenes of bands stepping out of their tour bus, and I wanted so badly to experience that moment. I still want to live that moment. In fact, it's still one of the small side requests I have for God.

I often think, *Jesus, I love the life you have given me. I love where you have led me and the dreams you have given me to fulfill. But is there a chance, at some point, we can throw a tour bus into the mix?*

Okay, sorry for the rabbit trail. But that's why forgiveness has to become a way of life. It will always be something we intentionally choose, or else we will revert back to blaming and discontent.

Have you ever been there? It is so much easier to wallow in self-pity and anger, blaming the person who hurt you, than it is to trust the unbeaten path of forgiving those who have hurt you. Whether or not they ask for forgiveness, whether or not the injustices are ever made right on this side of eternity, forgiveness is the choice we make to stop punishing ourselves and each other.

Maybe you have your own triggering "tour bus" moments that remind you of what happened to you and the dream you so needed to make you feel okay. If you are not careful to continually choose forgiveness, these triggering moments will perpetually steal your joy. These moments spoil your satisfaction with God's presence and provision in the moment you're in right now and decompose your gratitude. Before you know it, seeds of bitterness can take root.

> Work at getting along with each other and with God. Otherwise you'll never get so much as a glimpse of God. Make sure no one gets left out of God's generosity. Keep a sharp eye out for weeds of bitter discontent. A thistle or two gone to seed can ruin a whole garden in no time. (Hebrews 12:14–15)

Don't let seeds of bitterness ruin the garden of your soul and steal your future from you. If you're not careful, you will find yourself continually harvesting the pain of your past instead of reaping the sweet fruit of God's faithfulness. As Erwin McManus says, "Hope is always found in the future." That is where you are headed, and hope is what God's grace and provision bring.

Once again Joseph gives us some footsteps to follow in this difficult journey of forgiveness, once he was the governor of the land. He had been on an amazing journey up to that point. He was given a dream early in his life. Betrayed by his brothers and sold into slavery, that dream died. He experienced the amazing faithfulness of God, then was wrongly accused and imprisoned for years. Then, once again experienced the amazing faithfulness and redemption of God, being granted freedom and placed in charge of all of Egypt. But then all of these ups and downs, setbacks and setups, brought Joseph to possibly his greatest moment yet.

Quick backstory: A severe famine had spread across Egypt and the surrounding nations. God had granted Joseph favor in the eyes of Pharaoh and the wisdom to lead the country through that difficult time. It was his job to hand out grain to all those who came needing food during the famine.

Then Joseph's brothers arrive in Egypt needing grain.

At first when Joseph saw his brothers, he recognized them but pretended to be a stranger. He spoke harshly to them. "Where do you come from?" he asked.

"From the land of Canaan," they replied, "to buy food."

Although Joseph recognized his brothers, they did not recognize him. When he remembered his dreams about them, he said to them, "You are spies! You have come to see where our land is unprotected."

"No, my lord," they answered. "Your servants have come to buy food. We are all the sons of one man. Your servants are honest men, not spies."

What happens next is a full circle moment. Just like his dream foretold years earlier, his brothers bowed down to him with their faces to the ground. Then he remembered his dream. He had a choice to make.

If you read the whole story in the book of Genesis, chapters 42–45, you will be glad you did. I'll give you the short version. Joseph plays some mind games with his brothers for a minute; he doesn't reveal to them who he is. He gives the brothers time to reflect on what they've done and come face-to-face with their need for forgiveness.

Then the story culminates in this epic moment:

> Then Joseph could no longer control himself before all his attendants, and he cried out, "Have everyone leave my presence!" So there was no one with Joseph when he made himself known to his brothers. And he wept so loudly that the Egyptians heard him, and Pharaoh's household heard about it.
>
> Joseph said to his brothers, "I am Joseph! Is my father still living?" But his brothers were not able to answer him, because they were terrified at his presence.
>
> Then Joseph said to his brothers, "Come close to me." When they had done so, he said, "I am your brother Joseph, the one you sold

into Egypt! And now, do not be distressed and do not be angry with yourselves for selling me here, because it was to save lives that God sent me ahead of you. For two years now there has been famine in the land, and for the next five years there will be no plowing and reaping. But God sent me ahead of you to preserve for you a remnant on earth and to save your lives by a great deliverance.

"So then, it was not you who sent me here, but God. He made me father to Pharaoh, lord of his entire household and ruler of all Egypt." (Genesis 45:1–8 NIV)

Oh man, this story just keeps getting better! Joseph finally has his chance to get even! He is in charge of everything in Egypt. He has so much power and authority. He has the power to send his brothers who betrayed him to jail or probably even have them killed! This is big! What would you do?

If you ever find yourself in this type of moment, there is a very important truth that's important to remember. Your story and your dream are not the only ones that matter.

I can totally identify with Joseph in this moment. In the moments I chose forgiveness, I experienced the peace and freedom that forgiveness brings. Then something would happen and I remembered my dream and the process would start again. The emotions would return. The what-ifs would haunt me once again.

In those moments when it is hard to trust that God is at work and has only our best interest in mind, when we "remember our dreams," we must also remember God's faithfulness through the ages. This kind of remembering allows us to stay in the center of grace.

If God is the author and perfecter of life, if he really saw you and choose you before you were born, then you are a gift to the world, which doesn't just include your story. Walking in his dream means saying yes to his story. Your choices matter, here and now, both in your own story and in the grand story of the world for generations to come.

The MVPs of God's story—people like Joseph—walk with humility, grace, and servanthood. What amazing grace Joseph displays in this moment. Thank God that Joseph chose forgiveness to give us all a model for living out our calling in a spirit of grace and forgiveness.

Joseph's choice to forgive was the very thing that allowed him to experience the resurrection of his dreams. He chose forgiveness and experienced peace, purpose, and passion for the heart of God. He chose forgiveness, and his family experienced reconciliation and redemption. And those things are always, always, always the path of God.

What prepared Joseph's heart for this moment? I believe he chose to focus on the faithfulness of God instead of focusing on the unfaithfulness of people. This is why we are encouraged:

> Therefore, since we are surrounded by such a great cloud of witnesses, let us throw off everything that hinders and the sin that so easily entangles. And let us run with perseverance the race marked out for us, fixing our eyes on Jesus,

the pioneer and perfecter of faith. For the joy set before him he endured the cross, scorning its shame, and sat down at the right hand of the throne of God. Consider him who endured such opposition from sinners, so that you will not grow weary and lose heart. (Hebrews 12:1–3 NIV)

When we fix our eyes, our attention, our emotions, and our forgiveness on Jesus, we can't help but see his faithfulness. That is his character. We see his grace. His faithfulness and grace always outshine and overcome the pain and unfaithfulness we experience at the hands of other human beings. Nothing has happened to you by another human that God can't heal, overcome, and redeem through you.

God is the God of *what is*, not *what if*. If we continue to look backward and say, "What if…," we will never be ready to move forward and seize the day to discover what God is doing now. Forgiveness is the pathway into what is and what could be.

Forgiveness is a nonnegotiable if we want to live in freedom. To trust the heart of our Father enough to forgive means a future filled with moments where our dreams come to fulfillment more beautifully than we could ever orchestrate.

And do not bring sorrow to God's Holy Spirit by the way you live. Remember, he has identified you as his own, guaranteeing that you will be saved on the day of redemption. Get rid of all bitterness, rage, anger, harsh words, and slander, as well as all types of evil behavior. Instead,

> be kind to each other, tenderhearted, forgiving
> one another, just as God through Christ has for-
> given you. (Ephesians 4:30–32 NLT)

This is the standard, and it's a pretty amazing one at that. We are to forgive one another, just as God has forgiven us. "Just as?" Whoa. That is a high bar.

He doesn't ask us to do anything he hasn't already done. No one has more spiritual authority than God has in the world, yet he uses that authority and power to heal, forgive, make things new—and make us new.

Joseph's observance of God's faithfulness paved the way for him to offer forgiveness to his brothers. Focusing on God's faithfulness to forgive us truly empowers us to forgive others.

There is no record in Scripture of the exact internal process Joseph went through to find forgiveness for his brothers. We are only privy to the results—a family mended, peace restored, relationships healed, and mistakes redeemed.

He didn't forget it.

He forgave it.

He sent his brothers back with food, clothes, gifts, and even donkeys, and he instructed them to come back with their father and their possessions and said that he would provide a place for all of them to live so they could survive the remaining five years of famine. Yet, remembering his brothers' tendencies as he did, he sent them off with the exhortation: "Don't argue with one another on the trip home!"

Imagine having the power to either provide a new life for all of your brothers and their families or to get revenge. But what would Joseph have gained by retaliating? The brothers did, in fact, bow to him, just as he dreamed. His forgiveness both saved their lives and humbled them.

Years later, one of the closing images we have of Joseph and his brothers happens after their father, Jacob, dies. Even then, his brothers start to freak out, because they are worried that Joseph might feel free to bring on the revenge they deserved once their father was gone. They assumed Joseph may have still been festering rage in his heart. They even sent him a message reminding him that before their father died he had made the following request:

"Please forgive your brothers for the great wrong they did to you—for their sin in treating you so cruelly." When Joseph received the message, he broke down and wept. Then his brothers came and threw themselves down before Joseph. "Look, we are your slaves!" they said.

But Joseph replied, "Don't be afraid of me. Am I God, that I can punish you? You intended to harm me, but God intended it all for good. He brought me to this position so I could save the lives of many people. No, don't be afraid. I will continue to take care of you and your children." So he reassured them by speaking kindly to them. (Genesis 50:16–21 NLT)

This wasn't a case of sweeping the betrayal under the rug. Joseph didn't minimize it or didn't pretend it didn't happen. His focus wasn't on how he was wronged. His focus was on how faithful God was through his own pain, betrayal and confusion. Their choices could not stop the plans of God.

Were their moments when Joseph was sitting for years in prison for being wrongly accused that his emotions got the best of him and he hated his brothers for putting him in this situation? We don't know, but I'm going to go out on a limb and say there probably were.

Joseph was human just like you and me. Surely Joseph felt anything we would feel in that situation. The processes of grief and mourning are universal, so it's wise to assume Joseph processed through the cycle. The other reality is that this is not often a linear process. We may experience a looping, overlapping, and recycling of emotions from one day to the next. One day you may think you're through the process, and then something happens and you feel like you are back at step one.

Wherever you find yourself today, what matters most is that you know that forgiveness is a process. As you process your grief and own the journey of healing from the death of a dream, helpful survival skills are allowing compassion for yourself and giving yourself generous grace. The journey toward forgiveness is a road paved with grace. Grace for yourself as you heal. Grace from God as you heal. Grace for others as you heal. Grace for your denial. Grace for your anger. Grace for your bargaining. Grace for your depression. Grace for your acceptance. Grace for your not knowing where to go or what to do next.

In this process grace is best understood as presence. God's grace doesn't just forgive us, cancel our debts, and reconnect relationship with him. Grace invites us in and keeps us connected to the presence of God. I see it like a cycle of grace and forgiveness. God's grace ushers us into the cycle. It is grace that allows us to experience the forgiveness of God. Then grace shifts and reveals his presence. Then God's grace in us gives us the power and presence we need to heal and to be made ready to forgive. It is God's presence that empowers us to make the decision to forgive. Once we have forgiven, we are more able to be in the presence of those we are forgiving.

There are some unique situations where reconciliation or reestablishing presence with someone is impossible, unwise, or even unsafe. In cases of abuse, assault, or other scenarios where forgiveness and grace are not enough to break the cycle of trauma, removing yourself from the presence of the person who hurt you is the only viable option. You may, by God's grace, forgive an abuser while also understanding that cycles of abuse are not broken or healed with forgiveness alone. Patterns like these are complicated and I would not recommend anyone stay in a situation where you are unsafe.

If you have experienced the death of a dream by the actions of someone close to you who has already passed from this life, forgiveness is possible but reconciliation is impossible on this side of eternity, because reconciliation is a two-way street. Thank God, you can always choose forgiveness, which is a one-way street, even if the other person cannot or will not reciprocate or apologize. We are invited to forgive just as we have received forgiveness. But we cannot reconcile every broken relationship. Expecting reconciliation after forgiving someone can even get us stuck in bitterness when we are not able to experience reconciliation.

It's easy to make the mistake of believing that if we forgive someone we can still trust them or can immediately become their best friend again. Forgiveness does not promise an open door to friendship and reconnection.

Forgiveness is about releasing a debt. It is not a promise of reestablishing a relationship. It can, over time, free you from fear, anger, bitterness, and angst. But it doesn't mean you're endorsing the other person or establishing the level of trust you once enjoyed.

Joseph's lavish forgiveness of his brothers personifies the beatitudes from Matthew 5 that started this chapter, including this one from The Message translation: "You're blessed when you can show people how to cooperate instead of compete or fight. That's when you discover who you really are, and your place in God's family" (v. 9).

If you have experienced the death of a dream, this is your journey. This is your journey of healing and forgiveness. Just know that you do not have to do it alone. I don't know how anyone survives the death of a dream without knowing that God's grace is sufficient enough, that his plans are steadfast, and that you can trust him enough to release the people who have hurt you, just as you have been released from your own sins and wrongdoing.

As you discover who you really are and renew your trust in the promises God makes to all of us, you are changed from the inside. Then, and only then, you are ready to change your world.

## Chapter Sixteen

# PASSION AND PAIN

*We aren't punished for our sins, but by them.*
—Elbert Hubbard

When we suffer, it's easy to assume we are being punished by God. In reality, sin disconnects us from our Source, which is what creates the real pain. I used to think that sin was the big and obvious stuff that I learned early in life to avoid, like murder, adultery, and stealing. But even those obvious things start with tiny little decisions that disconnect us from our Source. Things like letting anger fester into bitterness, then hatred. Or letting selfishness grow in place of gratitude and trying to soothe our longing for significance with things that ultimately just bring on more pain.

Sin is often the result of trying to avoid pain and creating our own solutions. Slowly and deceptively, those self-made solutions disconnect us from the divine love we need more than anything else. I can see why Adam and Eve thought a little bite of fruit in the garden was no big deal. But it was an act of distrust that ultimately caused a fracture in their connection to their Creator. That small seed—thinking they knew better than God what was good for them—grew into a legacy of pain we still feel today.

God's dreams are derailed whenever we decide we know better than he does. The momentary pain of identifying what it is we're trying to avoid doesn't hold a candle to the pain we bring on ourselves by disconnecting from the very Source of passion, creativity, and hope. It is that disconnection and our desperate attempts to fix it ourselves that brings so much pain into our lives—our passion fizzles, our relationships suffer, we try ineffectively to control everything and everyone, we self-sabotage, and we do a million other futile things that ultimately make us feel isolated and miserable.

I hate pain. Who doesn't? But running away from it, patching it up with our own solutions, or trying to numb it just makes everything worse. Surrendering our pain to the God of love and inviting him into it is the only way for a story of pain to be transformed into a story of passion. Only then can we finally see our dreams as a creative collaboration with the greatest Healer of all time.

Researchers asked a group of kindergarten students for all the artists to raise their hands. One hundred percent of the kindergarteners raised their hands. The same researchers went into a third grade classroom and asked the same question. This time the number of kids who raised their hands decreased to about 50 percent. Next, they went into a sixth grade classroom and asked the same question. Less than 10 percent of the sixth graders raised their hands.

In kindergarten, we were artists! Our creativity, wonder, and imagination flowed effortlessly. Whether or not we demonstrated any prodigious skill or talent, creativity was just something we knew felt right. But what happened between kindergarten and sixth grade? You could conclude that those years revealed a natural progression of becoming more aware of our abilities and limitations. That may be true, but I would also add that kids begin to experience the pain of rejection, comparison, and failure, and begin to believe the voices of other people telling them who they are.

Jesus told his disciples, who were comparing themselves and asking him who was the greatest, that we simply must become like children, which means we need our imaginations intact. We need that sense of wonder we had before we started believing lies and the resulting disconnection they bring. Many of us lose the ability to dream while we are still kids.

How many people walking around this world actually feel fully alive? Maybe we start our lives with imagination but end with regrets. We regret becoming disconnected, which caused us to stop listening to our hearts. We regret not taking risks. We regret not living with a vision for what might be possible. These regrets happen when we lose our passion.

Maybe you have forgotten that you were born to create. Maybe no one's ever given you permission until now. Maybe you never realized what your gifts or abilities are. I would say it's safe to assume that we all need our dreams to be reignited at times. John the Baptist explains what Jesus desires to do in Matthew 3:11–12 when he says:

> I'm baptizing you here in the river, turning your old life in for a kingdom life. The real action comes next: The main character in this drama—compared to him, I'm a mere stagehand—will ignite the kingdom life within you, a fire within you, the Holy Spirit within you, changing you from the inside out. He's going to clean house—make a clean sweep of your lives. He'll place everything true in its proper place before God; everything false he'll put out with the trash to be burned.

I love this image John gives us of God's Spirit as fire. I love fire in general. Fire gives us the ability to see in the dark. Fire makes vision possible when there's nothing else to go on. I love the fact that fire purifies and refines and can even be used as fuel to propel us forward.

The bottom line is that Jesus wants to reignite your dreams. He wants so much to replace that pain with a fiery, passionate, illuminated life.

The passion you're longing to unpack in your own story means discovering who God has created you to be and connecting with his heart for you. You can trust his love, his character, and his promises.

I want you to know who you are. But even more than that, I want you to see who he is. I want you to understand your spiritual DNA and your voice in the world, but even more than that I want you to believe that he can transform your pain into passion in ways you can never accomplish alone. I want you to know the strengths and abilities you have, but I also want you to know his strength and his ability to weave together a story that will take your breath away. I want you to discover what makes you totally unique from the rest of the world's seven billion people, and I want you to see how irreplaceable you are in his dreams for the world. I want you to be confident and make an impact where you serve, knowing that it is he who ignites passion in you when you are connected to him as your Source. This is where passion leads you.

Imagine fire and passion in place of shivering alone with a cold, dead dream. This is the passionate life that it's unlocked when you begin to understand your spiritual DNA and trust the heart of a passionate God who has amazing dreams planned out for each of us.

Creating your future begins by looking in the rearview mirror of life at all the threads that may seem unrelated at first. Remember, it's all being woven; none of it will be wasted. What moments have brought you the greatest joy? What makes you laugh? What makes you cry? What keeps you up at night and brings you to your knees? Is there something that makes you sit on the edge of your seat when you talk about it? Pay attention to the places where your pain and passion intersect, and you may begin feel something resurrecting in you.

In the work I now do with people to help them discover their spiritual DNA, I start with helping them discover their unique calling. Ephesians 4:11 reveals that God has gifted each of us with one of five types of callings. Your APEST or Fivefold Calling will equip and empower you to discover how your personalities, gifts, and abilities intersect with God's dreams for the world. The five types of callings are apostle, prophet, evangelist, shepherd, and teacher. You can discover your unique God-given calling at www.SpiritualDNA.me.

Time and time again throughout Scripture, we see how God meets people in their pain, ignites their passions, and invites them to join him in what he wants to do in the world through them. In his great love, his dreams for us always far exceed what we ever thought possible when pain and disconnection threatened to take our lives off the rails.

Even Jesus's own story mingles passion and pain. The prophet Isaiah prophesied the arrival of Jesus hundreds of years before he showed up in the manger, and his words reflect how passion and pain come together in Jesus's life mission:

> For to us a child is born, to us a son is given, and the government will be on his shoulders. And he will be called Wonderful Counselor, Mighty God, Everlasting Father, Prince of Peace. Of the greatness of his government and peace there will be no end. He will reign on David's throne and over his kingdom, establishing and upholding it with justice and righteousness from that time on and forever. The zeal of the Lord Almighty will accomplish this. (Isaiah 9:6–7 NIV)

It is the zeal or passion of God that accomplished the mission of Jesus. For us to see our dreams reignited and to protect their fire, we must live a zealous and passionate life. Now let's look at the passion and the pain of two very famous gardens. The first garden is the one we read about in the very first pages of the Bible. It's a story of paradise lost and dreams being extinguished.

The story is a very familiar one, where the serpent comes to the garden and tempts Adam and Eve to distrust the character and the promises of God. Those temptations can be summarized by three lies. One, that God would not protect Adam and Eve. Two, that God would not provide for them. And three, that God would not approve of them.

These are always the three lies that can take us down. Believing these lies causes us to distrust the heart of God. Jesus faced these same lies in the desert, and at some point—or at many points—we all eventually face the same three lies.

Henri Nouwen says that the lies we believe always come back to some version of:

- I am what others think and say of me.
- I am what I have.
- I am what I do or accomplish.

These lies can extinguish the flames of passion with the cold water of fear. And 1 John 4:18 (NIV) is clear about the role of fear in our life with Christ:

> There is no fear in love. But perfect love drives out fear, because fear has to do with punishment. The one who fears is not made perfect in love.

His passion for us drives out fear, and fear is the enemy of dreams. We fear we won't have enough. We fear that we won't be enough. We fear we aren't doing enough.

Believing these lies always leads to the pain of regret. And, sadly, the pain of regret has the power to put out the fire of our passion. The pain of regret comes into our life when the pain of making the right decision seems too great. So we compromise.

The pain of regret usually doesn't hurt at the moment of decision, but it hurts forever after the fact. Maybe you've experienced this feeling in everyday things, like when you reject the pain of disciplined workouts and taking care of your body. Initially, it always feels better to eat a cheeseburger or a whole sleeve of Double Stuf Oreos. But when you reject the pain of discipline for six months and your pants don't fit...yikes. Now you understand the pain of regret.

You seriously feel it when you believe the lie that you are what people think about you, and you retaliate against people's opinions, even their gossip and lies about you, by fighting fire with fire. But this is how fire can start blazing out of control and burn you and other people. This is how the death of a dream begins.

But there's a second garden, the Garden of Gethsemane, where fear and the pain of discipline almost become too much for Jesus to bear.

What we see in the Garden of Gethsemane is Jesus once again trusting the protection, provision, and approval of the Father. He chose the pain of discipline to the point of suffering when he carried our sin—even sweating drops of blood—yet he kept trusting the heart of his Father. His endurance of pain on our behalf unlocked the opportunity for anyone to experience the fire of his passion for us.

We have many more amazing images and accounts of Jesus's passion that we can emulate as we learn to become people of passion. We see Jesus's passion on display in John 2, when he clears the money changers out of the temple for turning God's house into a moneymaking scheme. In his passion, Jesus exclaims, "Zeal for your house consumes me" (v. 17). Zeal is defined as energetic and unflagging pursuit of an aim or devotion to a cause.

Jesus was not just fiery for the sake of show, and he didn't just lose his temper because he was angry. He was passionate about protecting his Father's house and his plans for the church. This story of him turning over tables offers a very different glimpse of Jesus compared to the images of a pale, meek-looking Jesus gently carrying a small lamb over his shoulders that I remember hanging on the wall of my Sunday school classroom when I was a kid. I love seeing this fuller picture of Jesus as someone who is also a passionate force to be reckoned with, whose love and passion burn bright for us. In addition to his gentleness, I love to picture a sweaty, messy-haired warrior who rolls up his sleeves and fights whatever doesn't belong in our life with strength, determination, and protection.

Following him doesn't mean estrangement from ambition and passion. In fact, it's the opposite. Really knowing Christ and living in connection to him leads us to a passionate, fulfilling, ambitious future. Jesus understood his calling and was zealous about it. Jesus knew his purpose and that knowledge fueled his passion. The same can be true of you.

I urge you to allow God to reignite passion and dreams with his fire if yours is barely flickering. There will always be pain in life, but God is the only place we can take our pain and have it transformed into passion. His love, healing, and forgiveness hold the power to light us up—for the first time or for the mil-lionth time. When the going gets tough, when people fail us, when we go off course or forget who we are, our Source never loses power.

Paul says in Romans 5:3–5: "We know how troubles can develop passionate patience in us, and how that patience in turn forges the tempered steel of virtue, keeping us alert for whatever God will do next. In alert expectancy such as this, we're never left feeling shortchanged."

The pain purifies and the passion illuminates. If you're feel-ing the pain of regret, maybe a character defect sabotaged one of your dreams. The answer is not to shrink back and live a passive life to escape the pain. The dreams God ignited in you will be purified as you accept pain's role in your story and keep fully living without fear.

As the passionate heart of God ignites perseverance, char-acter, and hope inside you, the resurrection of your dreams is inevitable. Those dreams may take a different shape, and they may require growth and maturity, but they will fit you perfectly as you become ready.

Pain that is surrendered and transformed into passion will become the greatest indicator of where God needs your extraor-dinary gifts in the future. Not only does God refuse to waste any of our pain, but he will actually use our greatest pain to purify our greatest passion. I've seen it time and time again.

This passion from pain journey makes me think of my friend Davey Blackburn, who experienced the unthinkable pain of his wife, Amanda, and their unborn baby being killed in a brutal home invasion. The pain of this moment threatened everything in Davey's life. There were moments when he didn't know if he could go on. Even in his darkest of days, when lies threatened to convince Davey that God had abandoned him, Davey let the fire of God purify, refine, and heal him rather than snuff him out. In time, Davey's pain ignited his passion to start an organization called Nothing Is Wasted. Now Davey helps people all over the world walk through the aftermath of unthinkable trauma. He talks with people, allows them to process their pain, and walks with them through the transformation of their pain into renewed passion.

The pain in all of our stories has the potential to help us discover more about who we're created to be. The journey of chasing and living our dreams, then watching them go up in flames, can become the very process through which new passions are born.

The painful death of my dream felt like the end. That pain was the beginning of my ability to empathize with the pain others feel whose dreams are dead or dying. Now that pain seems small when I compare it to the passion that was set aflame to help others resurrect new purpose and step into who they were always born to be. The pain of my confusion has been transformed into a passion to help you take the next step to purify, redeem, and fuel your future.

I wouldn't have believed it at the time, but pain is always more than an end—it always carries with it the potential to set your heart aflame once again. Whatever pain you've experienced, it has the potential to be transformed to passion in time.

## Chapter Seventeen

# THE COURAGE TO DREAM AGAIN

*The great danger for most of us lies not in setting
our aim too high and falling short, but in setting
our aim too low in achieving our mark.*
—Michelangelo

As I sit in Arizona writing this labor of love, I'm not just thinking about my story and my dream. The reason I'm doing this reminiscing is because of you. I may not know all the details of your story, but I know that if you're still with me in the final chapter of this book, you are serious about making sense of your dreams, regardless of what they've cost you. And believe me, I know how much courage it takes to dream again when your dreams have cost you dearly.

Most of us will never reach the greatest potential meant for us until our dreams are stripped down, tested, worked out, laid to rest, grieved, surrendered, and finally reborn. I do not take it lightly that dreaming again can feel vulnerable, maybe even undoable.

If you are afraid to dream again, I want to tell you that I'm sorry for every unfair thing that has happened. I extend to you my sincere respect for every scary thing you've done in the past or will do in the days ahead. I want to stand and applaud every courageous thing you do in search of the person you've been created to be.

*Where* you are is not *who* you are. All of the love, and personality, and gifts your Maker wove into your DNA from the beginning, before the foundations of the earth, are still inside you. And over time, as you build your character and learn how to navigate setbacks and challenges, remember that the same Joseph who found himself at the bottom of a cistern eventually became the most powerful man in Egypt.

I think it's easy to let fear begin to creep in. And it's important to get honest with ourselves about what we are actually afraid of. Don't run from the fear. Embrace the fear. Get compassionately curious about your fears. Let that journey lead you towards courage. You *had* a dream. That was the past. You *have* a mission that will continue far into the future.

My hope and prayer for you is that your life can now be measured in two halves. The first half is everything your dreams meant to you up until now. And the second half is how you will now walk into the mission that has always been meant for you.

Ephesians 2 expresses these two halves of life so well:

You let the world, which doesn't know the first thing about living, tell you how to live…We all did it, all of us doing what we felt like doing, when we felt like doing it, all of us in the same boat. It's a wonder God didn't lose his temper and do away with the whole lot of us. Instead, immense in mercy and with an incredible love, he embraced us…and made us alive in Christ. He did all this on his own, with no help from us! Then he picked us up and set us down in highest heaven in company with Jesus, our Messiah. (Ephesians 2:2–6)

No need to beat yourself up for what happened in the first half of your life. Shame is not helpful in the journey forward. Grace and truth? Yes! Shame? No. We are all in the same boat trying to make sense of life one day at a time. I wrote this book because I know what it felt like to be in that boat, trying so hard to keep paddling with no idea where it was all going.

I want you to be able to live the second half of your life knowing how it feels to be picked up and placed in the company of Jesus. He lived, died, and was resurrected to guarantee that you could be made new. You are forgiven of everything you've ever done. You are made on purpose and for a purpose. Today is the day you can begin to live in that reality. You have a future to create.

If you are ready to step into the second half of your life, Ephesians 2 invites you into it like this:

Now God has us where he wants us, with all the time in this world and the next to shower grace and kindness upon us in Christ Jesus. Saving is all his idea, and all his work. All we do is trust him enough to let him do it. It's God's gift from start to finish! We don't play the major role. If we did, we'd probably go around bragging that we'd done the whole thing! No, we neither make nor save ourselves. God does both the making and saving. He creates each of us by Christ Jesus to join him in the work he does, the good work he has gotten ready for us to do, work we had better be doing. (Ephesians 2:7–10)

If God doesn't waste a single moment of our lives, let's take his cue and get on with creating the future. He has been weaving together every tiny detail to invite us into his dreams on a scale so huge that it spans generations. He has a dream coat ready to place upon your shoulders, a yoke that fits and aligns with your spiritual DNA! You have already been given everything you need! It is already in you.

Everything we could ever need for life and godliness has already been deposited in us by his divine power. For all this was lavished upon us through the rich experience of knowing him who has called us by name and invited us to come to him through a glorious manifestation of his goodness. As a result of this, he has given you magnificent promises that are beyond all price, so that through the power of these tremendous promises we can experience partnership with the divine nature, by which you have escaped the corrupt desires that are of the world. (2 Peter 1:3–4 TPT)

Read that scripture again. Everything you could ever need to become who you were born to be is already in you. You already possess it because of your connection and relationship with Jesus. Your are fully equipped for your purpose as you experience partnership with the divine nature. This is describing the reality of your spiritual DNA. Wow—what a gift. What a reality.

It's go time! No more dead dream grave tending. The world needs you fully alive and present. And since you know that nothing will be wasted—even mistakes and whatever you thought was a lost cause—there's no need to be worried that you're going to somehow get it wrong. God is just going to keep weaving the masterpiece of your life and inviting you into his dreams for you.

I love this advice, which is often misattributed to Mark Twain but is nonetheless wise: "Twenty years from now you will be more disappointed by the things that you didn't do than by the ones you did do, so throw off the bowlines, sail away from safe harbor, catch the trade winds in your sails. Explore, Dream, Discover."

Think ahead and imagine what you hope to be remembered for when your life is over. Do you want your friends gathering around at your actual funeral and lamenting about the fact that once your dream died, you quit living, too? No. You don't.

You want the time you have left to matter. You were made for this. You don't want to be shrunk and defeated by fear. This is a time to take God seriously when he invites us into a divine partnership.

"Therefore go..." These two words begin Jesus's directive to his followers in Matthew 28:19 (NIV) as their instructions for when he was no longer there to communicate with them in person.

*Go, explore, dream, discover, move, begin, take the risk, start! Therefore go!*

Submit your significance to his sovereignty. Embrace grace and humility for your weakness. Leverage your strengths and calling.

Trust me. You already have exactly what you need to move forward and live out your mission. This is coming from the guy whose report card once said, "Talks too much. Can't stay on task." Now I literally talk for a living. He has made you for whatever dream he is weaving! Even still, it is going to take courage.

Know that you are in good company. So many of the people we all admire once faced the death of their dreams. But we rarely hear about that part! I have the privilege of interviewing people all the time about their dreams, and I'm always amazed at their stories of broken dreams—and their courage to keep going.

One of those people is NFL Hall of Fame football coach Tony Dungy, whom I have admired ever since he coached the Indianapolis Colts. When I asked him if he had ever experienced the death of a dream, he didn't hesitate for a second and said, "Absolutely!"

He went on to share the story of how he got his start. Things went great for a while. In high school, he wanted to be an athlete, and it happened. He wanted to be the quarterback of the football team, and it happened. He wanted to take his team to a state championship, and it happened. Then, he wanted to go to college on a scholarship, and not only did he play for University of Minnesota on a scholarship, but he was named Most Valuable Player at the quarterback position. Twice. He dreamed of playing quarterback in the NFL, and it was about to happen. And then…it didn't. He didn't get drafted.

"It was all happening…until it wasn't." Even for Tony Dungy! I felt seen.

Tony recalled what he learned from his parents: Living by faith means understanding that God always has a plan when ours don't pan out. So Tony didn't give up. He pivoted. He changed positions and eventually did make it to the NFL, but not as a quarterback. After five years in the NFL, however, he got cut. At that point, his dream was as dead as it could possibly be.

It was then, at only twenty-five years of age, that Tony got a call from Coach Chuck Noll and was invited to join his coaching staff. He couldn't have imagined becoming a coach at his young age. Many of the players on his team were older than he was, but he trusted God's imagination. Step by step and risk by risk, he continued to coach NFL football and carried the weight of his calling with integrity and class. In 2006, Tony Dungy became the first Black coach ever to win a Super Bowl. In 2016, he was inducted into the Pro Football Hall of Fame. The death of his dream became the resurrection of his purpose.

Martin Luther King Jr.'s name is synonymous with the words "I have a dream." But did you know his dream early in life was to be a pastor? He wanted to lead people spiritually. So, when he was nominated to be the leader of a small civil rights group, he almost turned it down. His pain and his passion were closely bound together, as is the case with so many remarkable dreamers—and his passion for human rights emboldened him to lead more people than ever would have walked into the doors of a church. Because of his courage to follow God's dream for his life and for the world, he was able to shine a light on injustices that few people were willing to talk about at that time.

King's voice has become an enduring building block we are still building on today. We still draw on his life and words, which challenge people to think differently and see one another from a different and godly vantage point. And though he is considered a hero now, he was hated by many people who were threatened by his message. Yet his courageous voice was a beacon of hope for generations of Black Americans who once felt powerless to believe a bigger story.

If ever faced with the question "Will you leave, too?" King never backed down. He paid the ultimate price for that dream. He may have been shaking on the inside, and his family may have begged him to play it safe so he didn't get hurt, but he was undeterred. The death of his dream actually resulted in his physical death—and cost his family years of life without him. His legacy is very much alive and has impacted more people than he might have ever imagined during his lifetime. His passion is timeless.

Ultimately, the choice every human being has to make, regardless of what we are called to do, is whether or not we will leave, too. Will we press on? Will we stay in the room with the Creator of our dreams and keep learning to let him set aflame new possibilities that go beyond ourselves or even our lifetimes?

As Michelangelo said, "The great danger for most of us lies not in setting our aim too high and falling short, but in setting our aim too low in achieving our mark." But when God is writing your story, you can trust his imagination. What if you really believed that you were created for a significant, effective, and instrumental life? What if you began telling yourself you were created on purpose and for a purpose? What if you could fully trust that you have been uniquely designed to fulfill a part of God's dreams for the world that has been planned for you since day one? It's not something you have to go find or discover in a galaxy far, far away. It's literally woven into you.

Jesus is ready to walk with you into the future if only you will have the courage to dream again, even after everything that's happened. Even with all your questions. Even after the death of a dream—especially after the death of a dream.

I knew writing this book was going to force me to face my own fear and sense of inadequacy. Writing is much harder for me than speaking. I needed to be alone. I knew I needed a space where I couldn't be distracted. I think I have the spiritual gift of distraction and wasting time. But I knew if it was just me and Jesus, I might be able to get this done. So I rented a cabin in the foothills of the north valley of Phoenix, and it was perfect. It had Old West decor and was just big enough for me and Jesus.

The moment I got there I set my stuff down and walked out onto the deck overlooking the valley. I breathed in the desert beauty. I had missed this place, this valley, these colors, these smells. This was my valley, my home for so much of my childhood.

I set up my computer and my Bluetooth speaker, ready to start the journey of writing this book, this story, this journey of becoming who I was born to be. Before I started, I wanted to take a few minutes to settle my mind and my spirit with some worship. I had just discovered Cory Asbury's *To Love a Fool— Rooftop Experience (Live)* album. I sensed this was where it all needed to start.

I set my iPhone to shuffle and took a deep breath. I was ready to get to work with the Lord. But like God does, like a great Father would do, he wanted to spend some time with me before we got to work. The first song to come on randomly from the album—but absolutely not randomly—was "Crashing In." I would strongly encourage you to download the song and listen to it as you read the rest of this chapter. You can thank me later. The beauty of the music, the lyrics and the desert landscape ushered me into a holy space. Cory began to sing about a God who loves him well. He marvels at the absurdity of grace and his sense of unworthiness to receive it. All of this love and grace crashing in to remove the weight of the world, the pain of his failures and bringing him into a holy place of peace with his heavenly Father. These words were what I heard first, as I started this journey of sharing my story of learning to trust the heart of the Father.

And I lost it. I don't cry often. But that song in that moment wrecked me. Here once again the Father was wooing me, reminding me, and assuring me that I am loved, I am wel-comed. I can enjoy his peace, his love, his plan when I con-tinue to walk yoked with him. As the next verse of the song rang out through the speaker, more tears poured out of my eyes like a river of gratitude spilling over the banks of my soul. As long as I have been yoked with Jesus, I've had nothing to gain, lose, show, or prove. I am with him. His presence and peace empowering me to overcome the fears of creating the future day-by-day with him.

Friend, fear is my enemy. Fear is your enemy. However, when we are with God we can choose courage, and we can choose to trust. We can trade our fear for faith and dive into the adventure of becoming who we were born to be.

The song kept playing. By the time I got to the last verse, I thought maybe I was done crying. I thought maybe I had heard enough from God. Maybe the moment was over. But then the words filled my heart and poured out of my eyes again.

I do believe in a God who has and does and will always love me well. How did I ever not trust him? How did I ever believe that he would ruin my life? But he didn't reject me for thinking those things. He wasn't ashamed of me. He didn't ruin my life. He didn't make it suck. He patiently fathered me, as he still does. He understood the fears of that little third grader whose dreams were just being born. He had compassion for the entire journey of growing up. Every adventure, every win, every loss, every dream, every thread was woven to lovingly allow me to become who I was born to be. It is a delicate thing. It is a beautiful and powerful yet wonderfully delicate thing to become who we were born to be.

There I sat, drinking in this wonderful, delicate, wise, compassionate, and holy moment with my Father. He was wrapping his arms around me and saying, "You're exactly where you're supposed to be. In my arms, In my will. I love you. Let's do this together."

What a moment. What a Father! And here's the good news: He's your Dad too. He's your Father. He is loving you well. He will continue to wonderfully, delicately, and compassionately lead you and grow you up to become who you were born to be.

If you are still in the grieving stage of the death of your dreams, that's okay. As you walk, yoked with Jesus, you are exactly where you are supposed to be.

If you are patiently waiting for the resurrection of your purpose, that's okay. As you walk yoked with Jesus, you are exactly where you are supposed to be.

If you are experiencing the joy of seeing a dream resurrected and you are anxious and fearful that it will die again, that's okay. As you walk with Jesus, you are exactly where you are supposed to be.

I believe in you, friend. I'm so honored you picked up this book. I am so humbled that you have allowed me to be a part of your journey, of your dream. You are going to be okay. You were made to do tough things. You're made in the image of God, and God does tough things.

You can make it through this and come out the other side stronger, wiser, and more passionate. The world needs this new version of you. Your world needs the wiser, tougher, more trusting version of yourself. This might be your Good Friday, but resurrection Sunday is on the way.

Can I pray for you?

*Father, I thank you for my friends that are reading this book. I thank you for their dreams. I thank you for the gifts and abilities you have created them with to fulfill their unique purpose. Father I know you know the pain that comes with the death of a dream. You know our pain. You meet us with compassion in our disappointment and brokenhearted confusion. You do not leave us or forsake us.*

*You have established a covenant with us Father. Standing on the promises of that covenant, I ask that you would protect and provide for my friend. I pray that they would sense you walking close to them in this season. I pray that you would heal their heart. I ask God that you would give them the courage to forgive. Overwhelm them with your love and all that you have done for them, and give them the power of your Holy Spirit to love others as they have already been loved and will always be loved.*

*Father, I pray that you would give them eyes to see the new that you want to do in and through their life. I ask that you empower them to be strong and courageous as they bring you the best of their life. I ask that you would expand their imagination for what is possible for them to do and be. I ask that you would expand their faith to believe that you want to entrust to them the visions and dreams that cur-*

*rently fill your heart and mind. I pray, God, that they would experience the joy of joining you in your dreams for the world.*

*Lord, I ask that you would awaken them to understand their worth and value in you. I know that when they know their worth, they will change their world. I pray that their world would be changed with the faith, hope, and love of Jesus.*

*Father, please awaken them to become who they were born to be through the righteousness of Jesus Christ.*

*In Jesus's name,*
*Amen!*

# ABOUT THE AUTHOR

D aron Earlewine is a passionate, catalytic, influential, captivating, dreamer. He serves as a pastor, speaker, podcast host, and entrepreneur. His mission is to awaken people to become who they were born to be. Daron has helped thousands of people discover their unique, God-given callings through Spiritual DNA, the online course and live workshop he created. He also hosts The Daron Earlewine Podcast and is the founder of Pub Theology, which shares the good news of Jesus Christ with Hoosiers in the pubs and bars of Indianapolis. Daron and his wife Julie of twenty years live in Indianapolis Indiana with their three sons, Cole, Ty and Knox.

# ADDITIONAL RESOURCES

Connect with Daron, subscribe to his podcast or book him to speaking at his website.

www.daronearlewine.com

It is time to resurrect your purpose. Today is your day to become who YOU were born to be. The Spiritual DNA online course is your next step. There are multiple course options available as well as coaching from Daron Earlewine. Don't wait, head over to the Spiritual DNA website today!

www.spiritualdna.me

# A free ebook edition is available with the purchase of this book.

**To claim your free ebook edition:**

1. Visit MorganJamesBOGO.com
2. Sign your name CLEARLY in the space
3. Complete the form and submit a photo of the entire copyright page
4. You or your friend can download the ebook to your preferred device

A **FREE** ebook edition is available for you or a friend with the purchase of this print book.

CLEARLY SIGN YOUR NAME ABOVE

**Instructions to claim your free ebook edition:**
1. Visit MorganJamesBOGO.com
2. Sign your name CLEARLY in the space above
3. Complete the form and submit a photo of this entire page
4. You or your friend can download the ebook to your preferred device

## Print & Digital Together Forever.

Snap a photo

Free ebook

Read anywhere

CPSIA information can be obtained
at www.ICGtesting.com
Printed in the USA
JSHW020820100922
30355JS00001B/10